TABLE OF CONTENTS

Dedication	4
About the Author/Chef	6
Measurement Conversion Table	8
Vegan Substitutions	9, 10
Bits and Pieces	12-25
Watercolors/Shades of Green	26-39
Naturally Drawn	40-54
Rough Sketch	56-64
Painted Picnics & Shaded Plates	65-81
Sponge Boards	82-97
Sweet Pigments	98-113
Artistic Flow	114-126

Dedication

This cookbook, first of many to come, is dedicated to everyone who has supported me in eating my food, cooking my recipes and enjoying every single bite. A special thank you to my close loved ones, for the motivation to write and share my food with the world.

Love,

The Creative Chef

About The Author

Born and raised in a military family, I grew up all over the world. Having the opportunities to try new things along the way. I grew up, the oldest of four, being in a military family, I was home most of the time with my siblings when my parents worked. I spent a lot of nights preparing dinner for the family. I used what I could find in the fridge and cabinets and at times I challenged myself by placing ingredients on the counter that you would never think to put in a dish, and I made something out of it, something delicious. I have had a passion for cooking since I was incredibly young and began officially cooking before the age of 12. I was self-taught, until deciding to go to culinary arts school to learn what I had not already taught myself. I attended Le Cordon Bleu, College of Culinary Arts, USA. Going to culinary school was so intriguing, I learned so many things, tried things I never thought I would, and I was challenged in ways that I had not challenged myself before. I fell deeper in love with creating food.

In my free time, outside of baking and cooking three plus meals a day, among other things for family, friends, teachers, neighbors and even strangers, I spent a lot of time doing art. Not only is the art of baking and cooking a passion of mine, but I love all forms of the arts. I love to create with my hands, using my creativity and putting my heart into it all. I love to sketch, paint, create digital art or combine a mixture of techniques, like using charcoal and watercolors…etc. I love the idea of presenting something beautiful. Not just on a plate but also on a canvas. I love to create and share everything I make with anyone and everyone. It fills my heart to be able to create, then to share with people. I love to challenge myself in everyway possible and learn everything that I can from every experience.

When the idea of creating this cookbook was whisking around in my creative mind, the inspiration was to use my plate as my canvas. A blank canvas, something to challenge me. The idea of creating something different and beautiful, out of nothing, is my inspiration for creating. Once created, sharing it with everyone around is what keeps me creating more.

EAT MY CANVAS

CONVERSION TABLE

Imperial	Metric
1/8 tsp	0.5 mL
¼ tsp	1 mL
½ tsp	2.5 mL
1 tsp	5 mL
1 tbsp	15 mL
2 tbsp	30 mL
1 fl oz	30 mL
¼ cup	60 mL
1/3 cup	80 mL
½ cup	125 mL
2/3 cup	165 mL
¾ cup	190 mL
1 cup	250 mL
1 gallon (Can)	4.5 L
1 quart (Can)	1.1 L
1 gallon (US)	3.8 L
1 quart (US)	950 mL

Imperial	Metric
½ oz	14 g
1 oz	28 g
2 oz	56 g
¼ lb	113 g
½ lb (8 oz)	227 g
¾ lb	340 g
1 lb (16 oz)	454 g

Vegan SUBSTITUTIONS

Many companies make vegan versions to our everyday foods, but understanding what options you have, can be confusing. Here is a little cheat sheet that gives you a few different options that you can use to substitute non-vegan for vegan foods, so if you choose, you may enjoy the delicious recipes in this cookbook.

Vegan SUBSTITUTIONS...

Milk: Soymilk, rice milk, oat milk, hemp milk, nut milks.

Cheese: Using vegan cheeses is best. Daiya vegan cheese shreds well and is great for using in recipes like pizza.

Eggs: Tofu for dishes other than baking. Baking dishes; you can use applesauce, pureed tofu, mashed bananas

Beef/Chicken Stock: Use vegatable stock or vegatable boullion cubes.

Butter: Vegan butter.

Yogurt: Vegan yogurt or non-dairy yogurts like soy, coconut and almond based yogurts.

Sour Cream: Non-dairy plain yogurt or silken tofu.

Mayonnaise: Vegan Mayonnaise.

Gelatin: Agar flakes or agar powder.

Honey: Liquid sweetners, though these vary in sweetness levels.

Sugar: Beet sugar, organic natural sugar, turbino sugar, date sugar or monk fruit.

Chocolate: Vegan options or non-dairy versions

Meat: There are various versions of vegan meats.

BITS & PIECES

Melon & Prosciutto — a Sweet & Salty Creation

PREP TIME: 10 minutes // COOK TIME: 10 minutes // YIELD: 6 Servings

INGREDIENTS

- Cantaloupe melon
- 1-pound sliced prosciutto
- 2 cups sharp white cheddar cheese
- tablespoons heavy cream
- Dash of white pepper

CREATION

1. Prepare Melon:
   a. Slice melon in 1 inch thick slices, removing peel
   b. Wrap each slice of melon in sliced prosciutto, leaving the ends of the melon uncovered.
   c. Using cast iron grill or grill, cook/grill the prosciutto wrapped melon until there is grill marks on both sides and the prosciutto is slightly crispy.
   d. Once done, cover to keep warm.

2. Prepare cheese drizzle:
   a. In small/medium saucepan, over medium heat, add heavy cream.
   b. Allow the cream to get hot before adding in cheese. Once hot, add in cheese, stirring constantly until mixture has become a creamy sauce-like texture. Remove from heat.

3. Add dash of white pepper, and drizzle over melon and prosciutto.

Fried Canvases & Picante so

PREP TIME: 5 minutes // COOK TIME: 10 min // YIELD: 6 Servings

INGREDIENTS

- Circular canvas prepared ahead of time
- Recipe on Page
- Picante sauce (salsa of choice)
- Recipe on Page
- Oil for frying

CREATION

- Remove seeds from avocados, add to large mixing bowl
  a. Remove skin and
  b. Mash avocados in bowl

Mini Palettes

PREP TIME: 10 minutes // COOK TIME: 5 minutes // YIELD: 8-10 servings

INGREDIENTS

Rye bread
Salt
Pepper
Extra virgin coconut oil
3 tablespoons honey
Extra honey for drizzle
6-8 Fresh Apricots

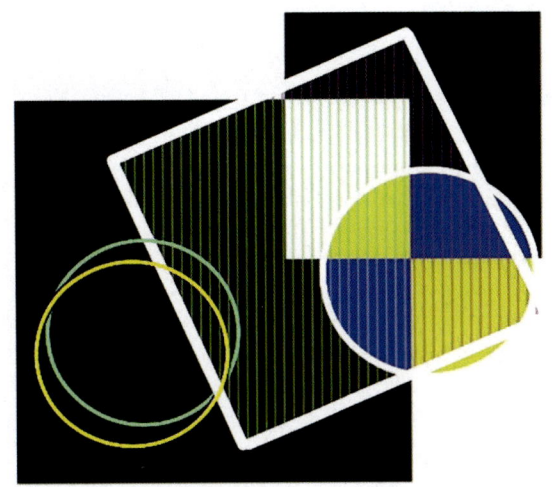

CREATION

1. Prep apricot drizzle:

a. Remove seeds and stems from apricots and dice apricots.

b. In small sauce-pan, add apricots and honey, cook mixture over low to medium heat until mixture breaks down a bit and begins to look more sauce like. Leaving mixture, a bit chunky in texture, remove from heat and set aside.

2. Prep crustinis:

a. Preheat oven to low broil.

b. Slice rye bread into thin slices. ¼ inch thick.

c. Brush oil on both sides of bread, coating surface well. (do not drench the bread in oil)

d. Place bread on baking sheet, sprinkle a generous amount of salt and pepper on each slice of bread.

e. Place in oven, broil (toast) until the surface is golden. Remove from oven, flip breads over and place back in oven to allow other side to toast as well. Remove from oven once other side is golden as well.

f. Drizzle apricot mixture over top of each slice of bread.

g. Drizzle honey over top of apricot mixture.

h. Serve right away.

Earth Capsacity

PREP TIME: 25 minutes // COOK TIME: 20-30 minutes // YIELD: 6-8 Servings

INGREDIENTS

2 cups Crustinis without the apricot/honey drizzle Recipe on page
8-10 baby portabella mushrooms or 4-6 large portabella Mushrooms
Extra virginCoconut oil
½ cup Sweet white wine
¼ cup diced shallot
2 cups fresh shaved parmesan cheese
1 egg
½ pound diced prosciutto
¼ cup honey
1 teaspoon red chili powder

Stuffed Mushrooms
Procuitto
Spicy Honey

CREATION

1. Prepare ahead of time, crustinis. Omit the apricot and honey drizzle. You only need the rye, salt and pepper toast for this recipe.

a. Once prepared, crush rye toast until it forms into crumbs, set aside.

2. Prepare mushroom filling:

a. In medium mixing bowl, add crumbs of crustinis, diced shallots and white wine. Mix until well mixed.

b. Add 1 egg and honey and mix well.

c. Set aside.

3. Prepare mushrooms:

a. Remove stalks from mushrooms.

b. Brush oil over entire mushroom, set on baking sheet.

c. Pre-heat oven to 350*F.

d. Fill mushrooms with filling.

e. Place in oven and cook for 20-25 minutes.

f. While mushrooms are in oven, prepare prosciutto.

4. Prepare topping:

a. In medium saucepan, cook diced prosciutto until crispy.

b. Remove from heat.

c. In separate bowl, add honey and red chili powder, mix well.

5. Once mushrooms are done, remove from oven, add crispy prosciutto to top of each mushroom, drizzle spicy honey on top. Serve hot.

Marked Canvaloupe & Salty Paper

PREP TIME: 10 minutes // COOK TIME: 10 minutes // YIELD: 6 Servings

INGREDIENTS

1 Cantaloupe melon
1-pound sliced prosciutto
2 cups sharp white cheddar cheese
4 table spoons heavy cream
Dash of white pepper

Melon & Procuitto

CREATION

1. **Prepare Melon**:
a. Slice melon in ½ inch thick slices, removing peel.
b. Wrap each slice of melon in sliced prosciutto, leaving the ends of the melon uncovered.
c. Using cast iron grill or grill, cook/grill the prosciutto wrapped melon until there is 'grill' marks on both sides and the prosciutto is slightly crispy.
d. Once done, cover to keep warm, set aside.
2. **Prepare cheese drizzle**:
a. In small- medium saucepan, over medium heat, add heavy cream.
b. Allow the cream to get hot before adding in cheese, once hot, add in cheese, stirring constantly until mixture has become a creamy sauce-like texture. Remove from heat.
c. Add dash of white pepper, and drizzle over melon and prosciutto.

Tri-Canvases & Picant-so

PREP TIME: 5 minutes // COOK TIME: 10 minutes // YIELD: 6 Servings

INGREDIENTS

1 Circular canvases recipe, prepared ahead of time
1 Pincant-so recipe (salsa of choice)
Oil for frying

Salt

Chips & Salsa

CREATION

a. Remove skin and seeds from avocados, add to large mixing bowl.
b. Mash avocados in bowl.
c. Add diced green onion to avocado and mix well.
d. Zest 2 lemons, add zest to avocado mixture, mix well.
e. Dice red grapes, add to mixture, combine until mixed.
f. Add salt and pepper, to taste.
g. Spread over toast of choice.

Browned Globes

PREP TIME: 25 minutes // COOK TIME: 20-30 minutes // YIELD: 6-8 Servings

INGREDIENTS

Beer batter
5 cups artichoke hearts
½ cup sweet white wine
1 cup sharp white cheddar cheese, shredded
½ cup shaved white chocolate
½ teaspoon red chili powder
Oil for frying

CREATION

1. Prepare wine cheddar drizzle:

a. In medium saucepan, add sweet white wine, over medium heat, allowing wine to cook down just a little, and so its hot.

b. Add white cheddar, stirring constantly until creamy in texture.

c. Add in red chili powder. Keep Warm.

2. Prepare beer batter and artichokes:

a. Once beer batter is prepared; preheat pot with oil or fryer to 375* F.

b. In small batches, drop artichokes in batter and fry until golden brown.

c. Once artichokes have been fried, drizzle wine and cheddar sauce over artichokes.

d. Sprinkle shaved white chocolate over top.

Fried Artichoke
Anise Beer Batter
White Wine
Spicy White Cheddar

Cubed Tart Globe

PREP TIME: 10 minutes // COOK TIME: 15 minutes // YIELD: 6-8 servings

INGREDIENTS

Wheel of Brie cheese
2 granny smith apples
1 bunch of chives, diced
1 package of bacon
1/3 cup Apple cider vinegar

CREATION

1. **Prepare pickled bacon and apple mixture:**

a. Dice apples; removing seeds, skin and stems, add into a bowl with the apple cider vinegar, set aside.

b. Dice bacon.

c. In medium saucepan, add bacon and cook over medium heat until bacon is close to being fully cooked and crispy.

d. Add diced apples and vinegar to bacon and continue to cook until bacon is crispy and apples are softer.

e. Remove from heat.

2. **Prepare brie:**

a. Preheat oven to 350*F.

b. Place wheel of brie cheese on baking sheet.

c. Over top of brie, add bacon and apple mixture.

d. Place in oven for 15 minutes to allow the brie to melt in the center a bit.

e. Once removed from the oven, sprinkle diced chives to top.

f. Serve hot.

Brie
Pickled Bacon
Green Apples & Chives

Pungent Circles

Onion Rings Thyme & Grape Dip

PREP TIME: 25 minutes // COOK TIME: 10-15 minutes // YIELD: 6-8 Servings

INGREDIENTS

1 cup flour (for beer batter)
1 cup flour (for prepping of onion rings) plus, 2 tablespoons cornstarch
1 teaspoon paprika
2 teaspoons salt
1 teaspoon white pepper
1 ½ cups Ale beer
2 large, sweet Vidalia onions
2 large egg whites
Oil for frying
2 teaspoons fresh thyme
1 teaspoon ground anise

FOR THE GRAPE DIP:

3 cups chopped ripe red seedless grapes
1 teaspoon lemon juice
1 zest of lemon
1 teaspoon fresh thyme
¼ cup diced purple onion
2 teaspoon honey
Dash of Salt & Pepper

CREATION

1. **Prepare Red Grape dip first:**

a. Start by chopping the grapes finely, add to mixing bowl.
b. Dice the purple onion and thyme, add to grape mixture.
c. Zest the lemon and juice the lemon, add to grape mixture.
d. Add 2 teaspoons of honey to bowl, mix until all ingredients are well mixed.
e. Cover and refrigerate until ready to serve/eat.

2. **Prepare beer batter and onion rings:**

a. In large bowl, mix dry ingredients, flour, salt, pepper and paprika and anise.
b. Chop thyme finely, add to dry mixture.
c. Whisk ale beer into mixture until smooth, if mixture seems too thick, add a little more beer.
d. In separate bowl, whisk egg whites until stiff peaks form.
e. Fold egg whites into beer batter until mixed but, do not over mix.
f. Set batter aside.
g. Remove skin and stems from onions and slice onions into ½ inch thick rings.
h. In separate bowl, add 1 cup flour and 2 tablespoons cornstarch, mix well.
i. Toss onion slices into cornstarch and flour mixture until onions are well coated.
j. In large pot or oil fryer, add oil, preheat oil to 375*F.
k. Once oil has reached desired temperature, in small batches, take floured onion slices and dip them in beer batter until fully covered in batter.
l. Drop onions into hot oil. Fry until onions are golden.
m. Once onion rings are done, sprinkle with a little salt. Serve with red grape dip.

Mossy Hearts

[handwritten: Spinach Dip, White Wine & Black Truffle]

PREP TIME: 10 minutes // COOK TIME: 10 minutes // YIELD: 6 Servings

INGREDIENTS

1 (8 ounce) package of cream cheese

½ cup mayonnaise

½ cup sour cream

1 minced clove of garlic

¼ cup minced shallot

¾ cup shaved, fresh parmesan cheese

1 teaspoon pepper

2 tablespoons white wine

1 cup artichoke hearts

1 cup fresh spinach, without stems

1 teaspoon shaved black truffle

CREATION

a. In medium-large sauce pan, add white wine, minced garlic and minced shallots. Cook 1-2 minutes on medium heat.

b. Add cream cheese, sour cream and mayonnaise, cook on medium heat, stirring constantly while cooking, to prevent mixture from burning; until mixture is creamy in texture.

c. Add artichoke hearts and parmesan cheese, mix in and cook over heat until cheese has melted.

d. Lower heat and add fresh spinach, cook until spinach is wilted. Usually this is very fast.

e. Remove from heat, add in shaved black truffle, mix well.

f. Serve hot.

Citrus Felt

PREP TIME: 5 minutes // COOK TIME: 0 minutes // YIELD: 6 Servings

INGREDIENTS

2-3 large avocados

1 cup diced green onion

Zest of 2 lemons

1 cup diced red, seedless grapes

Dash of salt & pepper

Avocado Spread Lemon & Grape

CREATION

a. Remove skin and seeds from the avocados, add in a large mixing bowl.

b. Mash avocados in bowl.

c. Add diced green onion to avocado and mix well.

d. Zest 2 lemons, add zest to avocado mixture, mix well.

e. Dice red grapes, add to mixture, combine until mixed.

f. Add salt and pepper, to taste.

g. Spread over toast of choice.

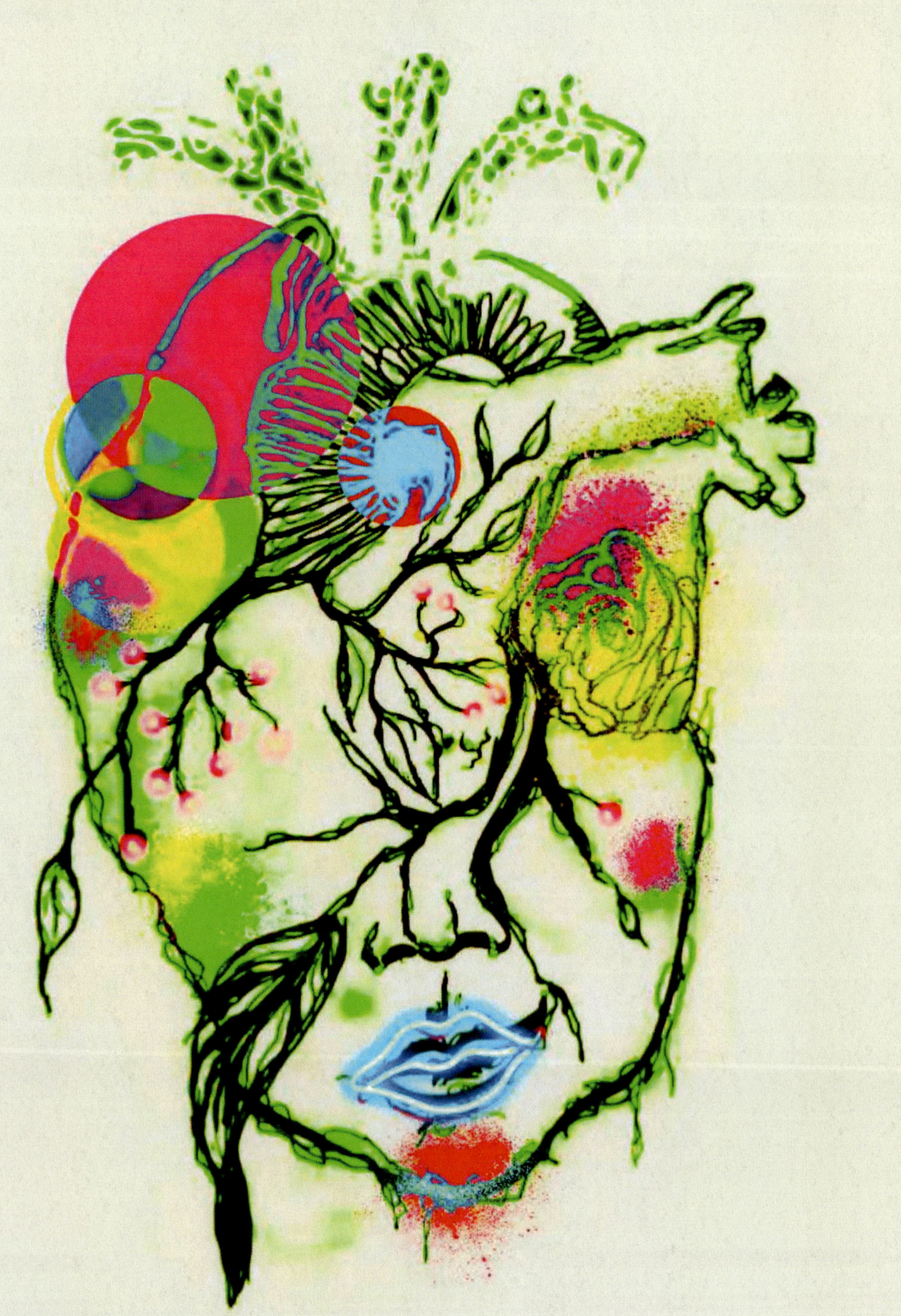

WATERCOLORS & Shades of Green

Artama-zing

PREP TIME: 10 minutes // COOK TIME: 0 minutes // YIELD: 6-8 servings

INGREDIENTS

6 cups arugula

1 cup fennel, sliced

2 full oranges, Supremes

Fennel & Arugula Salad Grapefruit & Honey Vinaigrette

INGREDIENTS FOR GRAPEFRUIT DRESSING

2 tablespoons shallot, diced

1/3 cup olive oil

1/3 cup white wine vinegar

½ cup grapefruit juice

1 tablespoon grapefruit zest

2 tablespoons honey

Dash of salt

Dash of pepper

CREATION

1. Prepare Grapefruit dressing:

a. Combine shallots, honey, white wine vinegar, olive oil, grapefruit juice, zest, salt and pepper into a jar.

b. Shake jar until all ingredients have emulsified together.

2. Prepare Salad:

a. Wash and place arugula on plate.

b. Slice fennel and toss with arugula.

c. Slice orange Supremes, fold in the salad.

d. Add dressing and toss until arugula is lightly coated.

Bak & Clouds

PREP TIME: 10 minutes // COOK TIME: 30 minutes // YIELD: 6-8 servings

INGREDIENTS

1 recipe of Apricot, onion Deo Rocks, NOT BAKED
1-pound chicken tenders, large diced
3 stalks of celery, diced

1 shallot, diced
3 carrots, diced
8-10 cups Chicken stock
2 tablespoons butter
1 teaspoon salt
2 teaspoons white pepper
1 teaspoon paprika
4 bay leaves

CREATION

1. Prepare Deo Rock recipe:
a. Make apricot and onion deo rock recipe, but do not bake. You will add the biscuit dough to soup later, set aside.

2. Prepare soup:
a. In large pot, add large- diced chicken and butter, cook until chicken is nearly cooked thoroughly.
b. Add celery, shallot and carrots and cook over medium heat for 5 minutes.
c. Add stock, if you need more liquid, you may add more stock or use water. Add bay leaves.
d. Bring to a boil, then reduce heat to medium low.
e. Add drops of deo rocks (apricot and onion biscuit dough) to hot soup, roughly ½ inch by ½ inch sized pieces. Cook until biscuit dough is fully cooked.
f. Remove bay leaves. Add salt, pepper and paprika; serve hot.

Shells in the Clouds

PREP TIME: 10 minutes // COOK TIME: 40 minutes // YIELD: 6-8 servings

Seafood Bisque Lemon & Candied Fennel

INGREDIENTS FOR CANDIED FENNEL

- 1 cup sugar
- ½ cup water

INGREDIENTS

- 2 cans of diced clams
- 2 (8 ounce) jars clam juice
- 2 cups heavy cream
- 6 cups vegetable stock
- Zest of 2 lemons
- 1 ½ cups sliced fennel
- 1 shallot, diced
- 3 tablespoons butter
- 1 cup crab, diced
- 2 stalks celery, diced
- 2 parsnips, diced
- 1 bunch chives, diced
- 1 cup scallops, diced
- 1 teaspoon salt
- 2 teaspoons white pepper
- 1 glove garlic, minced
- 1 teaspoon paprika
- 1 teaspoon ground nutmeg
- ½ teaspoon red chili powder

CREATION

1. **Prepare bisque:**

    a. Put butter in large pot, cook shallots and garlic clove until shallots are soft.

    b. Add all diced vegetables, except fennel and chives. Place in large pot. Cook on medium heat for a few minutes.

    c. Add stock and clam juice. Cook on medium heat until hot, light boil.

    d. Add clams, crab meat and scallops. Reduce heat to simmer 15 minutes.

2. **Prepare Candied Fennel:**

    a. In small saucepan over medium heat, add 1 cup of sugar, ½ cup of water. Bring to boil and boil for 10 minutes.

    b. Remove from heat. Toss sliced fennel in the simple syrup.

    c. Preheat oven to 350* F.

    c. Drain fennel, making sure fennel is coated completely with simple syrup liquid, place on parchment lined baking sheet.

    d. Place in oven and bake for 20 minutes or until fennel has 'candied'.

    e. Remove from oven.

3. **Prepare finished bisque:**

    a. Add heavy cream, simmer another 15 minutes until liquid is hot.

    b. Add white pepper, salt, lemon zest, ground nutmeg and chili powder.

    c. Let simmer 5-10 more minutes. Remove from heat. Serve hot, add diced chives and candied fennel over the top of finished bisque.

Prism of Colors *Rainbow Soup*

PREP TIME: 10 minutes // COOK TIME: 30 minutes // YIELD: 6-8 Servings

INGREDIENTS

1 yellow onion, diced
3 whole carrots, diced
3 stalks of celery, diced
4 red potatoes, diced
2 cups kale
1 cup, thinly sliced purple cabbage
Zest of one orange
1 cup yellow tomatoes, halved
8-10 cups chicken or vegetable stock
1 can black beans, strained and rinsed
Shaved parmesan (for topping)
½ teaspoon salt
1 teaspoon pepper
½ teaspoon paprika
4 bay leaves

CREATION

1. Prepare soup:

a. Dice and cut all vegetables, put carrots, onion, celery, potatoes, tomatoes, beans and bay leaves in large pot. Do not add, kale, cabbage and seasoning yet.

b. Add stock, if you need more liquid, you may add more stock, or water. Cook over medium heat until soup comes to a boil. Reduce heat to simmer until potatoes are cooked fully.

c. Once you turn heat off, while soup is hot, add cabbage, kale, salt, pepper and paprika. Remove bay leaves before serving.

d. Serve hot, add smoked cheese to top. This soup tastes amazing with crustinis. Recipe on Page

---

Blue Desert Blueberry & Cactus Soup

PREP TIME: 10 minutes // COOK TIME: 30 minutes // YIELD: 6-8 Servings

INGREDIENTS

5 cups Nopal cactus, diced
5 cups fresh blueberries
1 yellow onion, diced
2 stalks of celery, diced
2 parsnips, diced
1 teaspoon salt
1 ½ teaspoons pepper
4 bay leaves
8-10 cups chicken or vegetable stock
½ teaspoon ground cumin

CREATION

1. Prepare soup:

a. Cut all vegetables, put in large pot.

b. Add stock to pot, if you need more liquid, you may add more stock or add water.

c. Add bay leaves, cook over medium heat and bring to a boil.

d. Reduce heat to simmer, add blueberries, simmer for 15-20 minutes.

e. Remove from heat, add salt, pepper and paprika. Remove bay leaves before serving. Serve hot.

Lotus

Pickled Beets & Hardboiled Eggs Smoked Gouda & Cinnamon

PREP TIME: 25 minutes // COOK TIME: 20-30 minutes // YIELD: 6-8 Servings

INGREDIENTS

6-8 Hard-boiled eggs
5 cups arugula
1 ½ cups fresh red beets, large diced
1 cup shredded smoked gouda cheese
Drizzle of olive oil

INGREDIENTS FOR PICKLING LIQUID

1 ½ cup distilled white vinegar
1 ½ cup water
1 ½ cup sugar
2 tablespoons pickling spices
1 cinnamon stick

CREATION

1. Prepare hard boiled eggs, cool in ice bath. Peel eggs.

2. Prepare pickling liquid:

a. In medium saucepan, add sugar, vinegar, water. Bring to a boil. Remove from heat.

b. In heat safe jar(s), add pickling spices and cinnamon stick.

c. Add diced beets and hard-boiled eggs to jars.

d. Pour pickling liquid into jar(s) to fill completely. Put lid on jar. Chill completely.

3. Prepare salad:

a. After pickled egg and beets have completely cooled, remove egg and beets, slice both.

b. In large mixing bowl, add arugula, drizzle equal parts of olive oil and pickling liquid from jar, toss in arugula, using the oil and pickling liquid as the dressing. Only enough to coat the arugula lightly.

c. Place salad on plate, add sliced beets and eggs on top.

d. Sprinkle shredded smoke gouda cheese over salad.

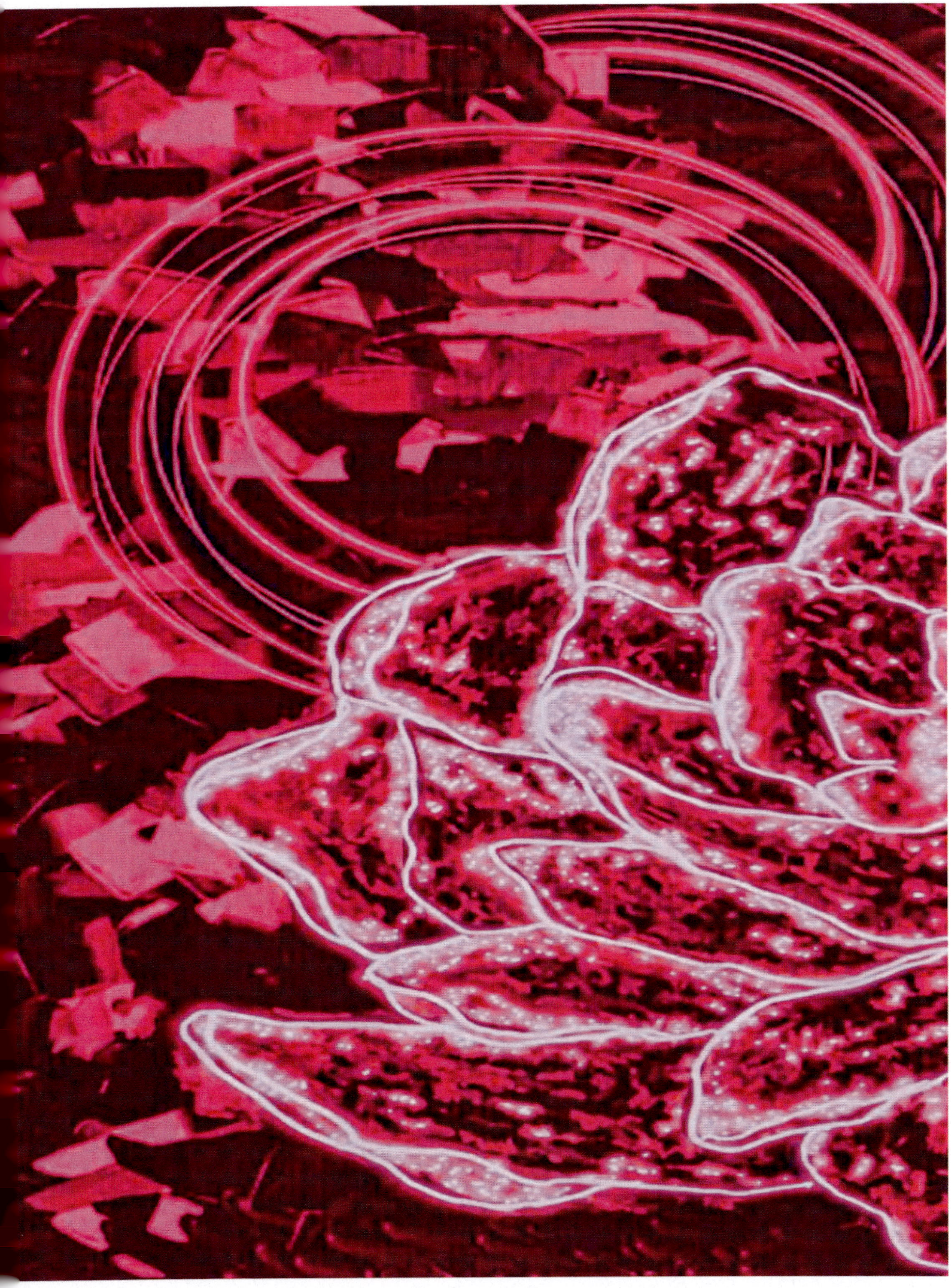

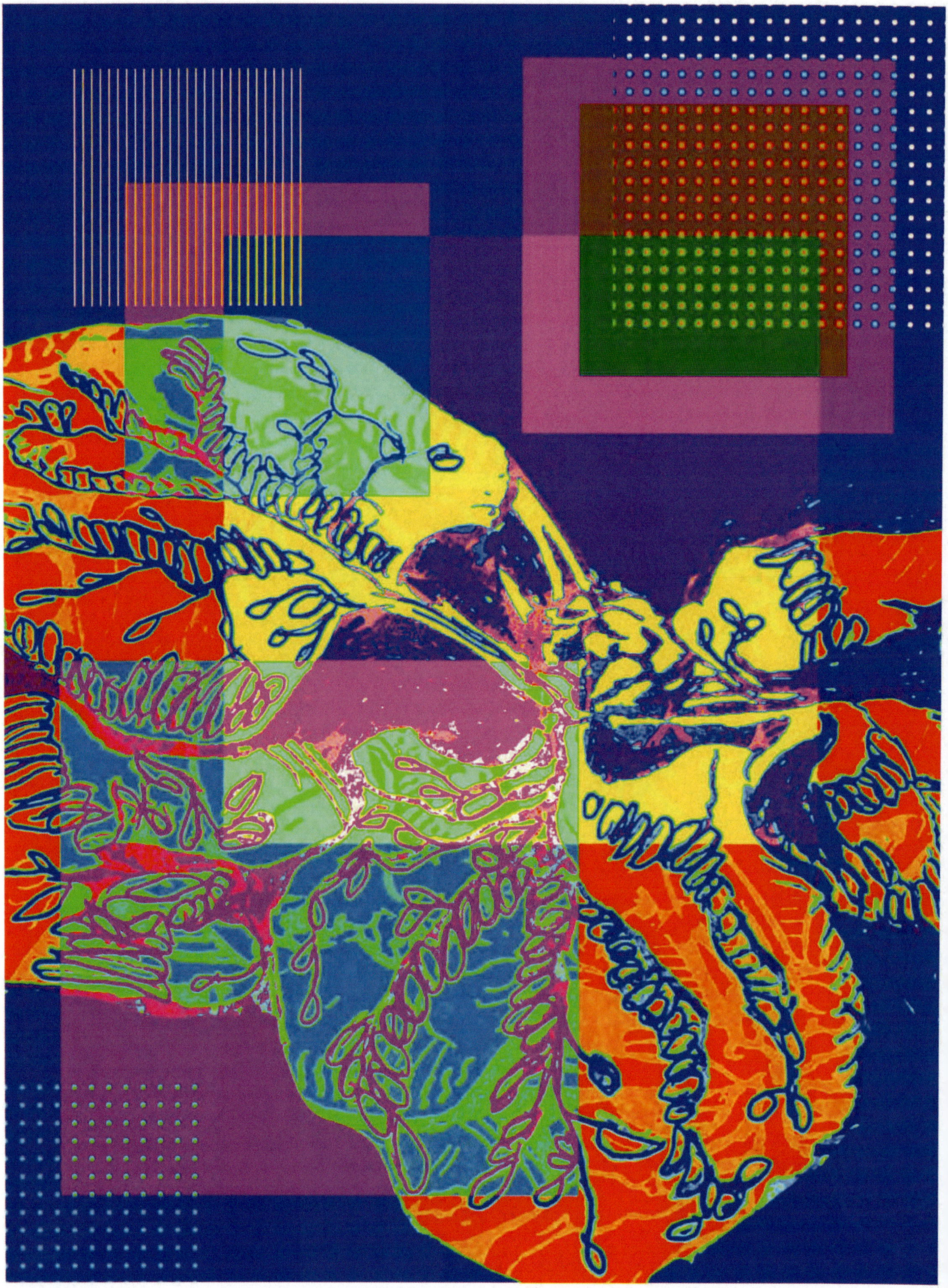

Ginger & the Beanstock

Ginger & Beansprout Soup

PREP TIME: 10 minutes // COOK TIME: 30 minutes // YIELD: 6-8 Servings

INGREDIENTS

4 cups mung bean sprouts
5 tablespoons fresh ground ginger
8 cups chicken or vegetable stock
1 yellow onion, diced
½ teaspoon salt
1 teaspoon pepper
1 cup canned or prepared northern beans
1 cup water chestnuts
2 parsnips, diced
1 garlic glove, minced

INGREDIENTS FOR CANDIED PANCETTA

8 oz fresh, sliced pancetta
¼ cup light brown sugar

CREATION

1. Prepare candied pancetta:

a. In medium saucepan, add diced pancetta and cook until crispy.

b. Add brown sugar and let simmer. Until sugar cooks down and creates a candied coating.

c. Remove from heat and set aside.

2. Prepare soup:

a. In large pot, drizzle olive oil and add garlic, parsnips and onion. Cook until onions are soft.

b. Add stock. Bring to a boil. Then reduce heat.

c. Add water chestnuts, beans and mung sprouts and fresh ginger; simmer for 10 minutes.

d. Remove from heat, add salt, pepper,

e. Put in bowl, serve hot and add brown sugar candied pancetta.

Pop-Ert

PREP TIME: 10 minutes // COOK TIME: 20 minutes // YIELD: 6-8 Servings

INGREDIENTS

6 cups fresh spinach
1 package smoked bacon, diced
2 tablespoons brown sugar
1 teaspoon cinnamon
½ cup pine nuts
1/2 teaspoon red chili powder
Dash of salt

CREATION

a. In large skillet, add diced bacon, cook until nearly crispy. Add brown sugar and cook until bacon is 'candied', over medium heat.

b. Add cinnamon and pine nuts, stirring often, reduce heat.

c. Add chili powder, mix.

d. Add fresh spinach and dash of salt. Cook until spinach has wilted. Do not over wilt. Remove from heat. Serve hot.

Not- Cold Spinach Salad Cinnamon & Spicy Red Pepper

Greens & Clay

Kale & Potato Blood Orange Soup

PREP TIME: 10 minutes // COOK TIME: 30 minutes // YIELD: 6-8 Servings

INGREDIENTS

5 large Idaho potatoes, diced
3 cups fresh kale
Zest of 2 blood oranges
Juice from 2 blood oranges
1 yellow onion, diced
2 stalks celery, diced
2 parsnips, diced
2 cups diced genoa salami
Shredded smoked gouda for top
8-10 cups vegetable or chicken stock
1 teaspoon salt
1 ½ teaspoon pepper

CREATION

a. Dice all vegetables and meat, place in large pot. Do not add kale yet.

b. Add stock, if you need more liquid, you may add more stock or water. Bring to a boil over medium heat, until potatoes are cooked through.

c. Add zest of blood orange, juice of blood orange and reduce heat to simmer for 10 minutes.

d. Remove from heat, add kale, salt and pepper.

e. Serve hot, add smoked gouda to top.

Sweet Vibes

PREP TIME: 15 minutes // COOK TIME: 0 minutes // YIELD: 6-8 Servings

INGREDIENTS

4 Fresh peaches
2 cups fresh basil
16 oz fresh mozzarella
1/3 cup olive
½ cup grapefruit juice
Zest of one grapefruit
1/3 cup white vine vinegar
3 tablespoon honey

Peach Caprese Honey & Grapefruit Vinaigrette

CREATION

1. Prepare Dressing:

a. Put grapefruit juice, zest of grapefruit, white wine vinegar, olive oil and honey in jar.

b. Shake jar until ingredients emulsify together.

2. Prepare caprese:

a. Remove seed and stem from peaches, slice in ½ in thick slices, lightly grill peaches until marked.

b. Slice fresh mozzarella in ¼ - ½ inch thick slices. Lay out on plate. Place sliced peaches over top of mozzarella.

c. Slice fresh basil and sprinkle decent amount over peaches and mozzarella.

d. Drizzle dressing over top of caprese.

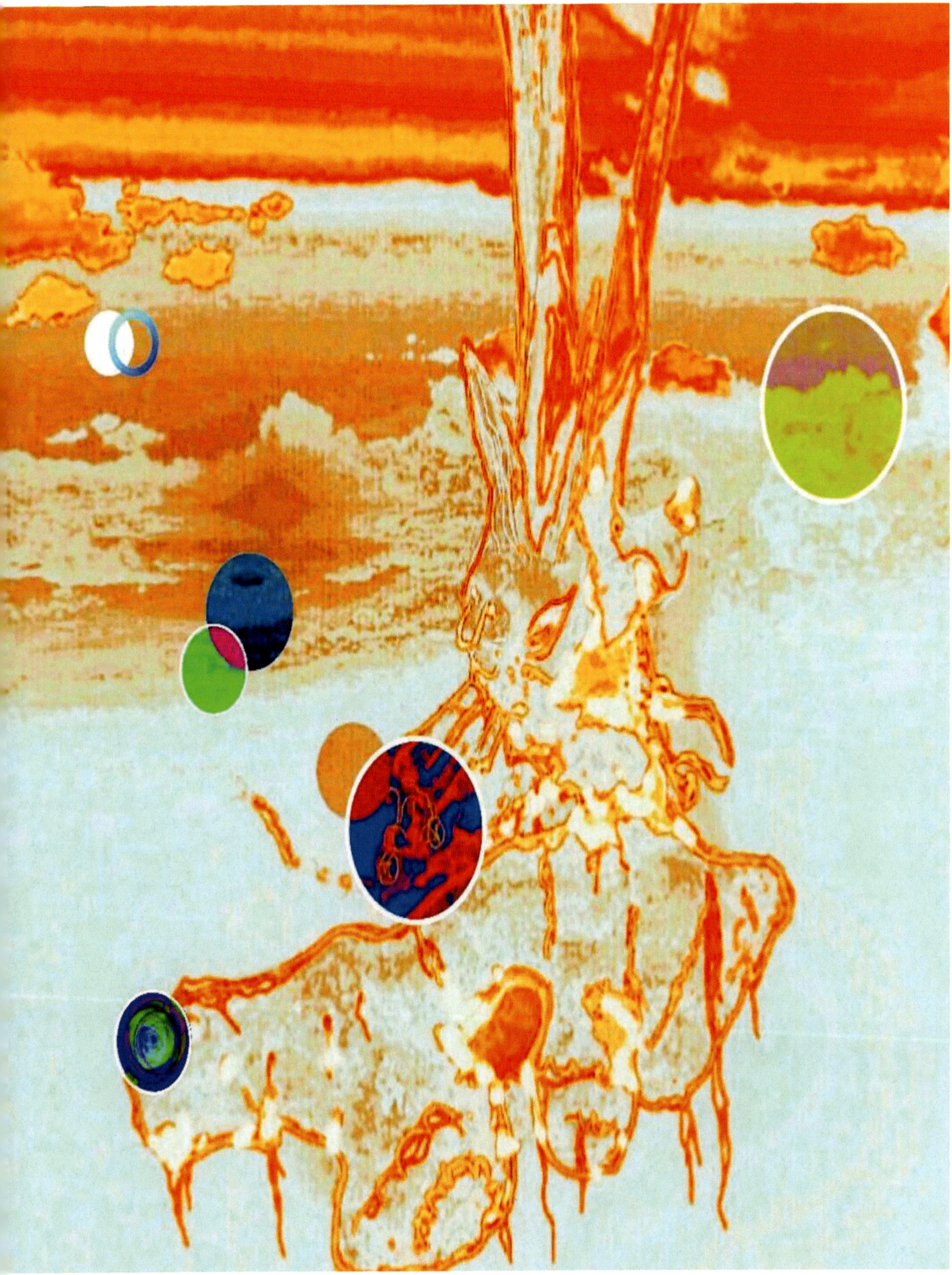

Naturally Drawn

1 egg

½ pound diced prosciutto

¼ cup honey

1 teaspoon red chili powder

Spicy Honey

CREATION

1. Prepare ahead of time, crostini's and the apricot and honey drizzle. You only need the rye, salt and pepper toast for this recipe

   a. Once prepared, crush rye toast until it forms into crumbs, set aside.

2. Prepare stuffing

   a. In medium sized bowl, add the bread crumbs, diced shallots and white wine. Mix until well mixed. b. Add 1 egg and honey and mix well.

   c. Set aside.

3. Prepare mushrooms

   a. Remove stalks from mushrooms.

   b. Brush oil over entire mushroom, set on baking sheet.

   c. Preheat oven 350°

   d. Fill mushrooms with stuffing.

   e. Place in oven and cook for 20-25 minutes.

   f. While mushrooms are in oven, prepare prosciutto

4. Prepare topping

   a. In medium saucepan, cook diced prosciutto until crispy.

Browned Globes

PREP TIME: 25 minutes // COOK TIME: 20-30 minutes // YIELD: 6-8 Servings

---

   b. Remove from heat.

   c. In separate bowl, add honey and red chili powder, mix well.

5. Once mushrooms are done, remove from oven, add crispy prosciutto to top of each mushroom, drizzle spicy honey on top. Serve hot

CREATION INGREDIENTS

1 Prepare wire cheddar drizzle

   Beer batter

   Recipe on page

   5 cups artichoke hearts

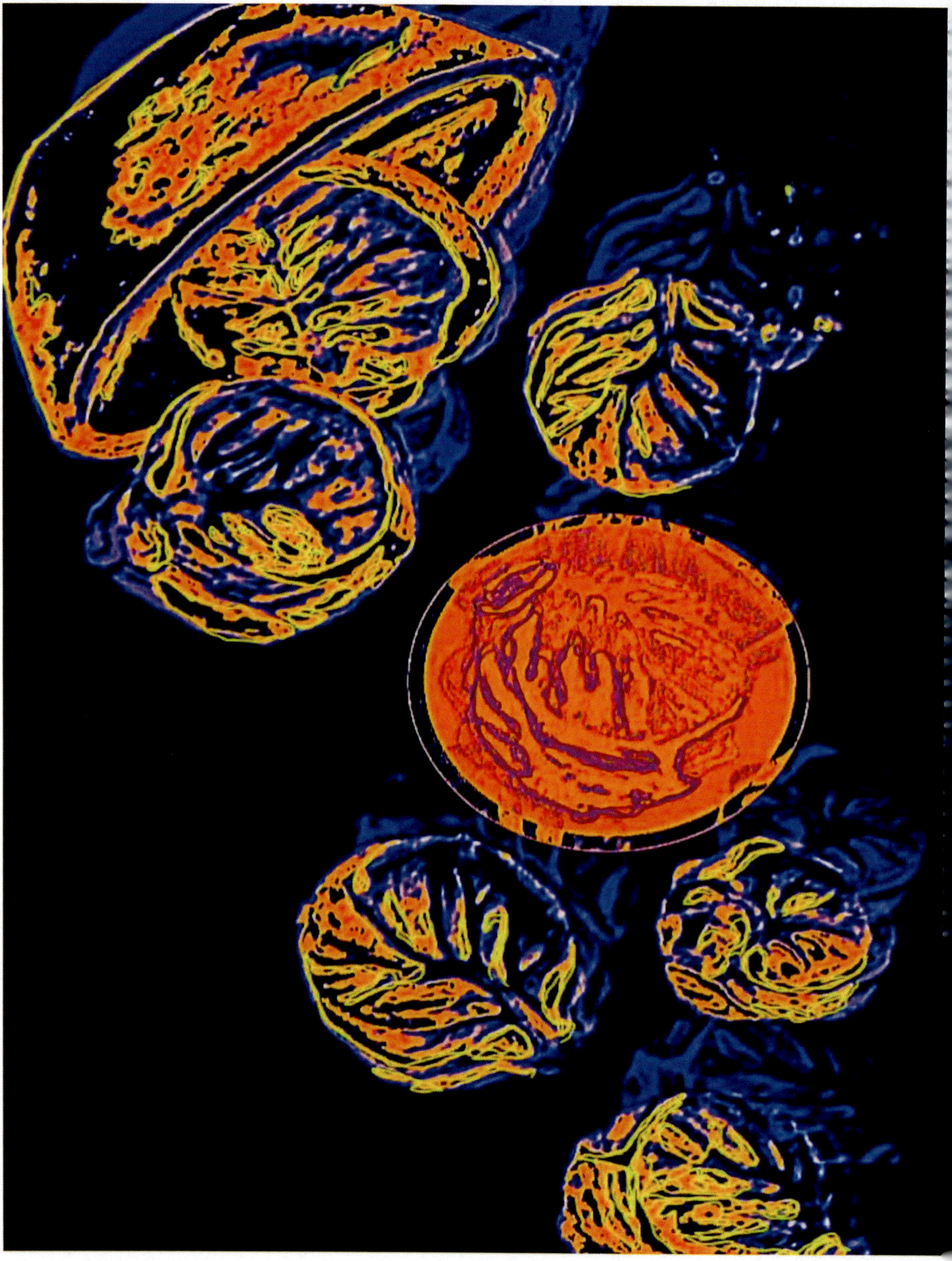

Savory Flowers

Sausage & Cabbage Blackberries & Sage

PREP TIME: 10 minutes // COOK TIME: 15 minutes // YIELD: 6 Servings

INGREDIENTS

4 cups polish sausage, sliced

3 cups green cabbage, sliced

1 cup fresh blackberries

½ cup fresh sage

1 teaspoon salt

1 ½ teaspoon pepper

5 tablespoons olive oil

CREATION

a. In large skillet, add sliced polish sausage. Cook until sausage is cooked thoroughly.

b. Add blackberries, cook until blackberries break down a tiny bit.

c. Add olive oil and sliced cabbage

d. Cook until cabbage is aldente.

e. Add salt, pepper and sage.

f. Remove from heat, serve hot.

Drunken Sprouts

Tarragon, Brownsugar Rum Brussel Sprouts

PREP TIME: 10 minutes // COOK TIME: 30 minutes // YIELD: 6 Servings

INGREDIENTS

2 cups fresh brussel sprouts, halved

2 large-sweet potatoes, large diced

3 tablespoons fresh tarragon, minced

1 teaspoon salt

1 teaspoon pepper

1 tablespoon brown sugar

1/4 cup dark rum

3 tablespoons clarified butter or extra virgin coconut oil

CREATION

a. Preheat oven to 375*F

b. On large baking sheet, line with parchment paper.

c. In large mixing bowl, add halved brussel sprouts, diced sweet potatoes.

d. In separate bowl, add oil, rum, tarragon, salt, pepper and brown sugar; mix well.

e. Pour liquid mixture over sweet potatoes and brussel sprouts, toss until mixture coats all brussel sprouts and sweets potatoes.

f. Place well-coated brussel sprouts and sweet potatoes in even layer on baking sheet.

g. Place in oven and roast until golden in color and potatoes are thoroughly cooked.

h. Remove from oven, serve hot.

Blistered Scrafts

Squash, Rosemary Bechamel & Honey

PREP TIME: 10 minutes // COOK TIME: 30 minutes // YIELD: 6-8 servings

INGREDIENTS

2 delicata squash, sliced

½ cup sliced fresh fennel

2 tablespoons fresh rosemary

1 cup pumpkin seeds

Honey for drizzle

2 teaspoons ground cinnamon

Oil for frying

INGREDIENTS FOR BECHAMEL

6 tablespoon butter

¼ cup flour

3 ½ cups half & half

1 ½ teaspoons salt

1 teaspoon white pepper

½ teaspoon ground nutmeg

CREATION

1. Prepare pumpkin seeds:

a. Preheat oven to 350*F.

b. Place pumpkin seeds in bowl and toss with cinnamon until coated with cinnamon.

c. Place on baking sheet and put in oven for 30-45 minutes. Until toasted. Remove from oven and set aside.

2. Prepare bechamel:

a. In medium saucepan, add butter and flour to make roux.

b. Cook butter and flour mixture, stirring constantly until flour has cooked and butter and flour mixture makes a ball that does not stick to the pan.

c. Whisking continuously, adding a small amount at a time, add half and half, until all half and half has been added. Continue to cook until mixture is creamy and thick in texture.

d. Remove from heat, add salt, pepper and nutmeg, mix. Keep bechamel warm for serving.

3. Prepare squash:

a. Slice squash in circular rings about ½ inch thick. Carefully removing seeds.

b. Preheat oil in pot or fryer at 375*F.

c. Adding in small batches, add squash rings to oil, fry until golden and blistered looking.

d. Remove from oil.

e. Finely dice fennel and rosemary, set aside.

f. Place squash on plate, drizzle bechamel over, drizzle honey, sprinkle fennel and rosemary over top and top off with cinnamon pumpkin seeds.

Silky Pearls

Mint Risotto, White Wine & Shallots

PREP TIME: 10 minutes // COOK TIME: 30 minutes // YIELD: 6-8 servings

INGREDIENTS

1 shallot, diced small
1 clove garlic, minced
4 tablespoons butter, unsalted
1 cup white wine
¼ cup fresh mint leaves, diced
4 cups chicken stock
1 ½ cup arborio rice
1 teaspoon salt
1 teaspoon white pepper
Dash of red chili powder
1 cup fresh shave parmesan cheese

CREATION

a. In saucepan, heat chicken stock until hot. Turn off heat.

b. In separate saucepan, add butter, shallots and garlic, cook over medium heat until shallots are soft and clear in color.

c. Add rice to shallot and garlic mixture. Mix well, still over medium heat for a couple minutes, to heat rice.

d. Adding a little at a time, add chicken stock to rice mixture, stirring constantly. Cook while stirring until rice has soaked up all of stock liquid. Repeat this until all stock has been eventually added.

e. Add white wine, simmer for 5 minutes.

f. Remove from heat. Add parmesan, salt, pepper, dash of chili powder.

g. Add minced mint leaf. Serve hot.

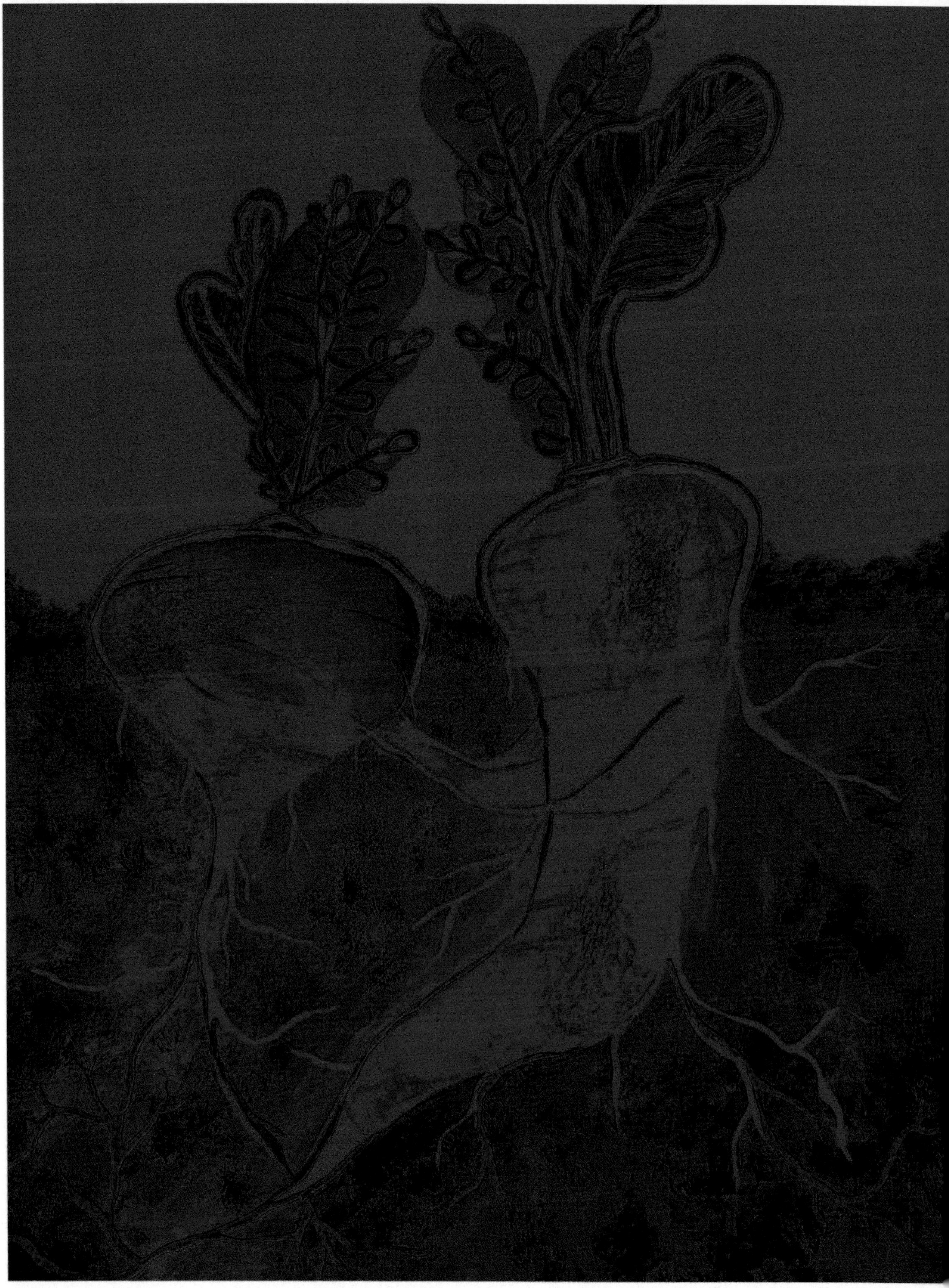

Sweet Roots

PREP TIME: 15 minutes // COOK TIME: 25 minutes // YIELD: 6-8 Servings

INGREDIENTS

1 cup golden turnip, large diced
1 large-sweet potato, diced
3 parsnips, diced
4 stalks celery, diced
1 yellow onion, diced
2 tablespoons fresh ginger, minced
½ cup leek, sliced
1 cup daikon, diced (or radish)
2 teaspoons salt
2 teaspoons pepper
1 teaspoon paprika
¼ teaspoon red chili powder
Extra virgin coconut oil to coat vegetables
½ cup honey

CREATION

a. Preheat oven to 400*F
b. Dice all vegetables, put in large mixing bowl. Except ginger.
c. Drizzle oil over vegetables and toss to ensure all vegetables have been lightly coated in olive oil.
d. On large baking sheet, line with parchment paper. Pour all vegetables in one even layer on sheet.
e. In small bowl, combine salt, pepper, chili powder and paprika.
f. Sprinkle seasoning over top of all vegetables, evenly.
g. In separate small bowl, add honey and ginger, mix.
h. Drizzle honey mixture over vegetables.
i. Place baking sheet in oven and roast vegetables until golden.
j. Remove from oven, serve hot.

Honey Glazed Root Vegetables

Herbed Layers

PREP TIME: 15 minutes // COOK TIME: 20 minutes // YIELD: 6-8 Servings

INGREDIENTS

1 tablespoon fresh rosemary
1 tablespoon fresh sage
1 tablespoon fresh thyme
3 large white onions
2 tablespoons olive oil
½ teaspoon salt
½ teaspoon salt

INGREDIENTS FOR WHITE CHOCOLATE DRIZZLE

2 Chocolate bars, baking white chocolate works BEST
2 tablespoons dry white wine
Dash red chili powder

CREATION

1. **Prepare onions:**
a. Preheat oven to 375*F
b. Slice onions in ½ inch thick rings, put in large mixing bowl.
c. Finely dice thyme, rosemary and sage.
d. In separate, small bowl, add olive oil, rosemary, thyme, sage, salt and pepper, mix.
e. Drizzle olive oil mix over onions, ensure all onion have been coated.
f. On baking sheet, line with parchment paper, place onions on baking sheet, in an even layer. While onions roast, make white chocolate drizzle.

2. **Prepare White chocolate drizzle:**
a. In small saucepan, break white chocolate into smaller pieces and add to saucepan.
b. Over medium-low heat, stirring constantly to prevent the chocolate from burning. Cook until melted.
c. Add white wine and reduce heat, continuing to stir constantly, cook for a few minutes, until wine is dissolved completely in white chocolate.
d. Remove from heat, add dash of red chili powder.

3. **Prepare final onions:**
a. Remove Onions from oven when edges on onions have turned golden.
b. Serve hot, drizzle white chocolate win sauce over onions.

Rosmary, Sage, Thyme Onions
White Chocolate

Coastal Mounds & Moddguepodge

PREP TIME: 15 minutes // COOK TIME: 45 minutes // YIELD: 6-8 servings

INGREDIENTS

- 6-8 red potatoes, skin on, large diced
- 1 ½ cup fresh scallops
- 2 tablespoons clarified butter (scallops)
- 3 tablespoons clarified butter (potatoes)
- 1 teaspoon salt
- 2 teaspoons white pepper
- Zest of two lemons
- 2 teaspoon sugar
- 1/3 cup heavy cream
- 1 Moddguepodge recipe

Mashed Potatoes
Sugared Lemon Zest
Scallops & Sage Gravy

CREATION

1. Prepare potatoes:

a. In large pot, boil potatoes until soft enough to mash. While potatoes boil....

2. Prepare scallops:

a. In skillet, over medium heat. Melt 2 tablespoons butter.

b. Add diced scallops until cooked through, do not overcook. Set aside.

3. Prepare moddguepodge recipe:

4. Prepare dish:

a. Once potatoes are cooked thoroughly, strain all water out.

b. Mash potatoes, leaving some chunks, or if you prefer it to be more mashed, mashed

c. Add butter, heavy cream. Mix well.

d. Add scallops, mix in well.

e. Add salt and pepper, mix well.

f. In small bowl, zest lemon and add sugar, mix well. Then add mixture to potatoes. Mix, well.

g. Plate potatoes, pour over desired amount of moddgguepodge (gravy).

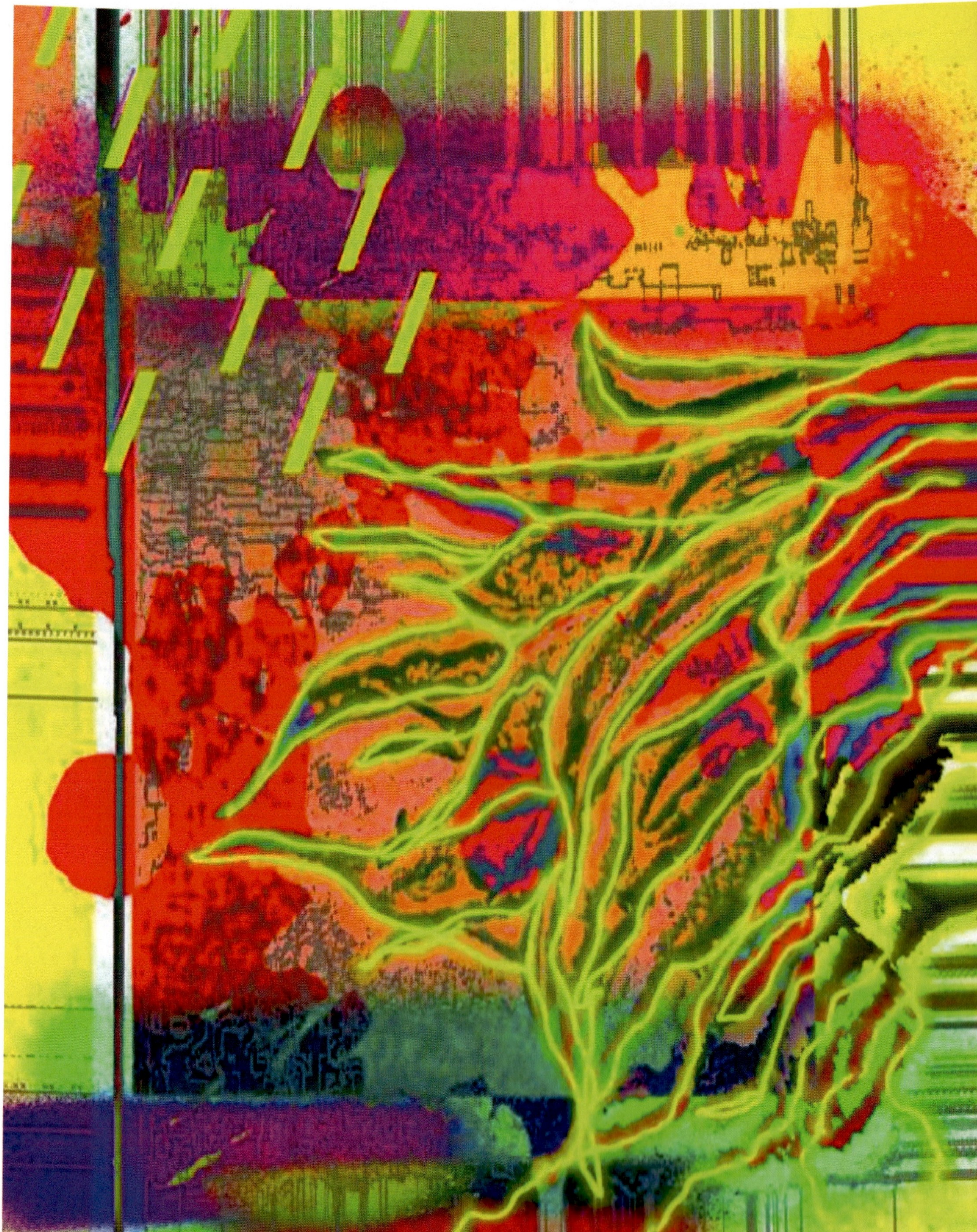

Frizzled Greens

PREP TIME: 10 minutes // COOK TIME: 15 minutes // YIELD: 6 Servings

INGREDIENTS

5 cups fresh French-style green beans
1 package smoked bacon
1 teaspoon ground anise
Olive oil for sauté
1 cup fresh red bell pepper, diced
dash of salt
½ teaspoon pepper

Greenbeans Red Peppers & Anise

CREATION

a. In large skillet, add diced bacon and cook over medium heat.

b. While bacon cooks, blanch green beans in boiling water and salt until green beans turn bright green in color, usually just a couple minutes. Then put green beans in ice bath (bowl of ice and water) to stop the cooking of the green beans.

c. When bacon has fully cooked, add diced red bell pepper, toss.

d. Add green beans, cook until red bell peppers are softer but still have a slight crunch.

e. Add ground anise, salt and pepper, toss.

f. Remove from heat. Serve hot.

Panned Stalks

PREP TIME: 10 minutes // COOK TIME: 30 minutes // YIELD: 6 Servings

INGREDIENTS

1 cup fresh leek, sliced
½ cup fresh fennel, sliced
1 cup white northern or navy beans (prepared or canned)
2 cup baby portabella mushrooms, whole
¾ cup dry white wine
1 tablespoon honey
1 teaspoon salt
1 teaspoon pepper
1 tablespoon butter, unsalted

CREATION

a. In large skillet, over medium heat, add butter. Melt butter.

b. Add leek, fennel and mushrooms. Cook for couple minutes

c. Add white wine and honey. Reduce heat, simmer until wine and reduces.

d. Add beans, cook few more minutes, until beans are hot.

e. Remove from heat, add salt and pepper. Serve hot.

White Wine Glazed Mushrooms & Fennel

Dressed Cobs

PREP TIME: 15 minutes // COOK TIME: 30 minutes // YIELD: 6-8 Servings

INGREDIENTS

6 Corn on the cobs
¾ cup mayonnaise
¾ cup sour cream
1 teaspoon ground cumin
1 teaspoon red chili powder
Zest of 2 limes
2 cups grated cotija cheese
(or grated parmesan)

INGREDIENTS FOR JALEPENO BLACKBERRY SAUCE

2 fresh jalapenos
2 cups fresh, whole blackberries
2 tablespoons honey
1 tablespoon water
Juice from 1 lime

Elote Corn Jalapeno Blackberry Drizzle

CREATION

1. Prepare Jalapeno sauce:
a. Remove seeds and stems from jalapenos, dice small.
b. Wash and add black berries and diced jalapenos to small saucepan.
c. Add water, cook over medium heat, bring to a boil.
d. Reduce heat and simmer until blackberries and jalapenos break down and become more sauce-like.
e. Remove from heat, let cool.
f. Blend in blender until smooth, add honey juice of lime; blend until well mixed. Set aside.

2. Prepare Corn:
g. In large pot, boil corn cobs in water and salt, until fully cooked. While corn boils make dressing.

3. Prepare dressing:
a. In mixing bowl, add sour cream, mayonnaise, zest of lime, ground cumin and red chili powder, mix well.
b. In saucepan, add dressing ingredients and cook on low heat until hot. Remove from heat.

4. Prepare Elote Corn:
a. Remove cooked corn cobs, brush with hot dressing to cover entire corn, then roll in cotija cheese, covering entire corn with cheese, drizzle with jalapeno/blackberry sauce.

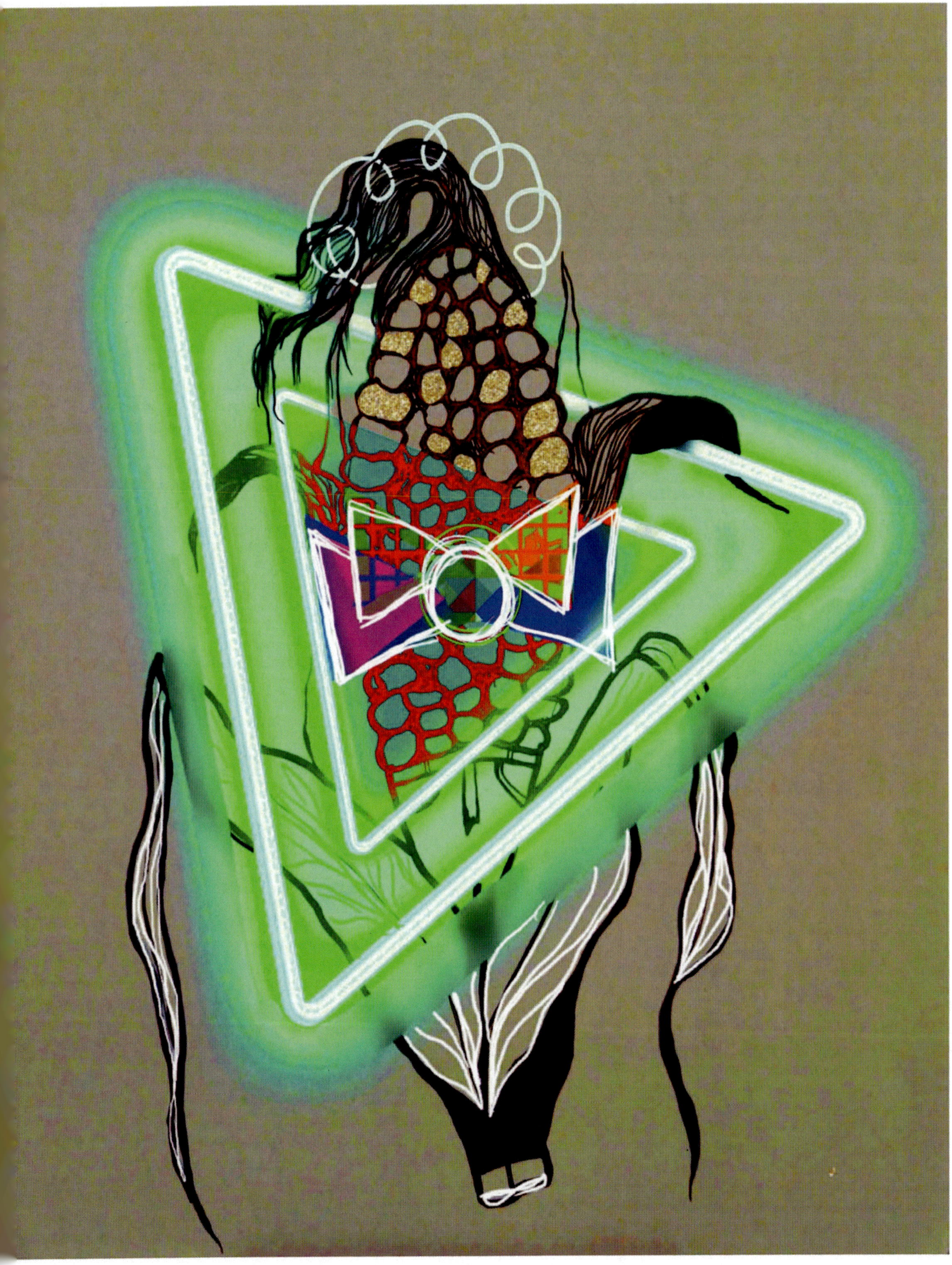

Brined Harvest

PREP TIME: 10 minutes // COOK TIME: 45 minutes // YIELD: 6-8 servings

INGREDIENTS

2 fresh whole jalapenos

1 fresh whole habanero

3 fresh pickling cucumbers

3 cups red Lentils

6 medjool dates, whole, pitted

3 tablespoons pickling spices

INGREDIENTS FOR PICKLING LIQUID

2 cups sugar

2 cups water

2 cups distilled white vinegar

Pickled Jalapenos Lentils & Dates

CREATION

1. Prepare pickled brine:

a. In large saucepan, add sugar, water and vinegar, bring to a boil.

b. while pickling liquid comes to a boil. In a large jar(s), add pickling spices. If using more than one jar, use the same amount of pickling spices per jar.

c. Add whole jalapenos, cucumber and habanero to jars.

d. When pickling liquid comes to boil, remove from heat, pour over vegetables in jars until completely emerged in liquid. Put lid on jar and refrigerate until cool.

2. Prepare lentils:

a. Rinse lentils well.

b. In large saucepan, fill halfway- ¾ full of water, bring to a boil.

c. Add lentils, simmer until lentils are soft. Remove and drain excess water.

3. Prepare full dish:

a. Once lentils are done, strained from water, leave in saucepan.

b. Remove pickled vegetables and peppers from, add small amount of pickling liquid to lentils.

c. Dice pickled vegetables, add to lentils and heat over medium heat until hot. Remove from heat.

d. Dice dates and sprinkle over lentils once plated.

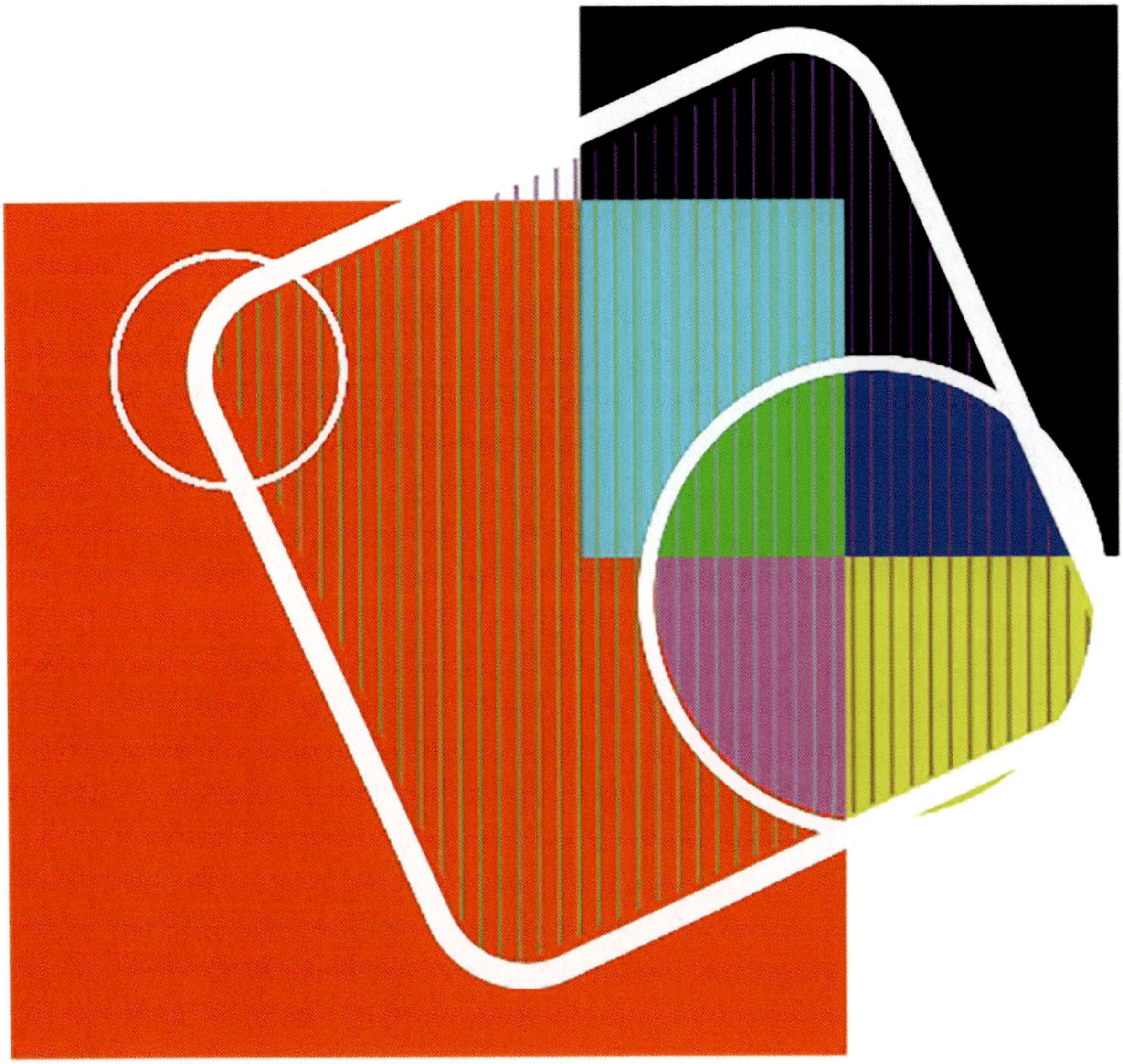

Rough Sketch

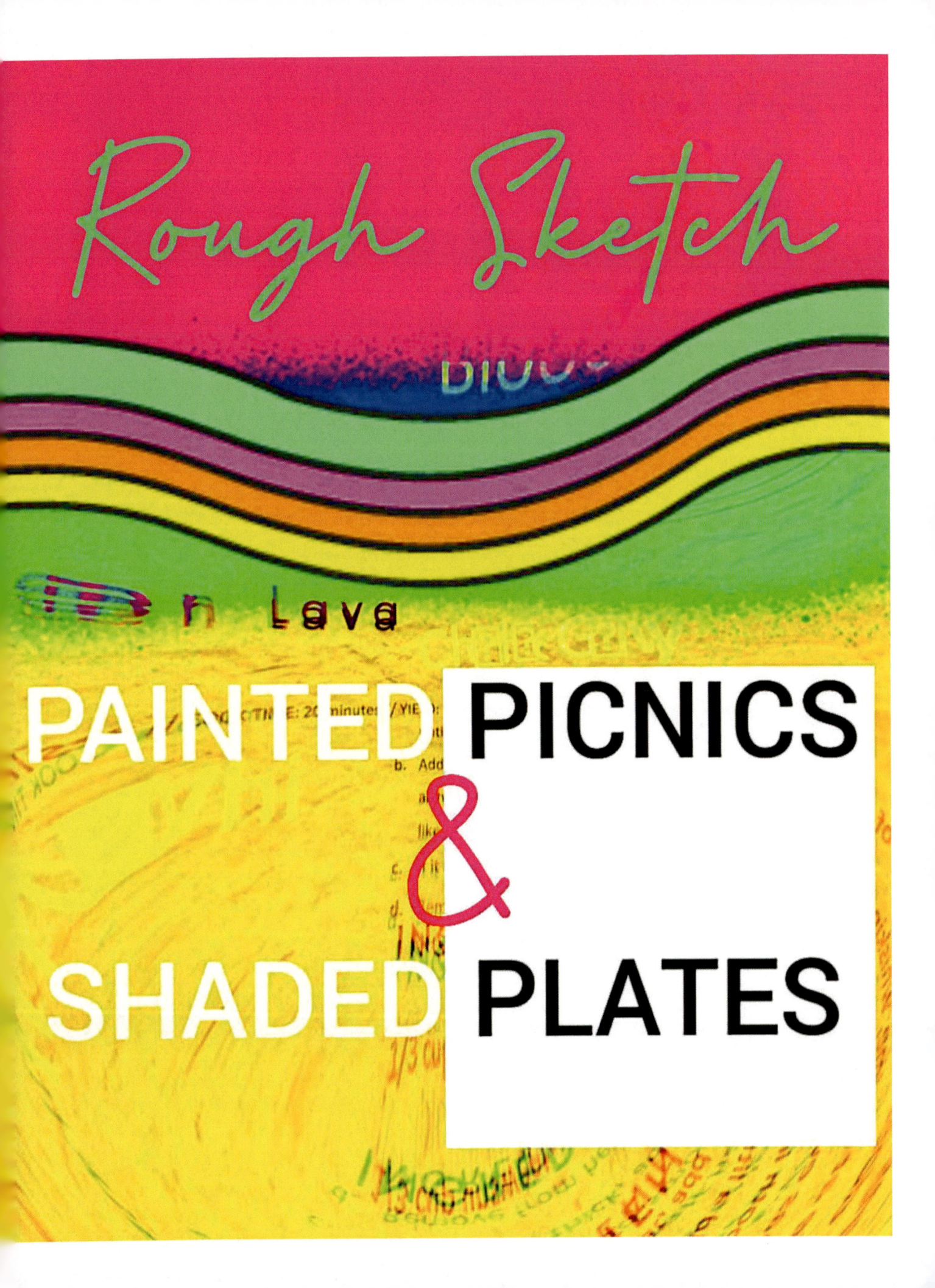

PAINTED PICNICS & SHADED PLATES

Sun-Out

Eggs Benedict Sage & Grape Pico De Gall (handwritten)

PREP TIME: 10 minutes // COOK TIME: 30 minutes // YIELD: 6-8 servings

INGREDIENTS

1 moddguepodge recipe (add 1/4 cup extra half and half, add 1 cup shaved parmesan cheese while sauce is hot, mix until cheese is melted and sauce is creamy)
6 -8 eggs
4 english muffins, split
6-8 slices of canadian-style bacon
3 teaspoons white distilled vinegar

INGREDIENTS FOR GRAPE PICO

1 cup red seedless grapes, diced
1 shallot, diced
2 teaspoons fresh sage, diced
¼ teaspoon salt
¼ teaspoon pepper

CREATION

1. **Prepare modgepodge recipe, set aside, but keep hot.**
2. **Prepare Grape pico:**
a. Dice grapes and shallots. Put in small bowl. Add salt and pepper and sage. Mix well, set aside.
3. **Prepare eggs:**
a. In large pot, bring 3 cups water to a boil over medium-high heat, add vinegar. Once it is brought to a boil, crack and drop eggs in the water, one at a time. You are poaching eggs. While eggs poach for a few minutes…(cook only until whites are fully cooked but yolks are yolky) Remove eggs with slotted spoon
b. Toast English muffins.
c. In frying pan, add Canadian-style bacon and cook until hot.
d. Plating, add one half, toasted English muffin, slice of Canadian bacon, and one egg, stacked.
e. Add moddguepodge recipe over top of stacked ingredients. Add spoonful of grape pico to top.
f. Serve hot.

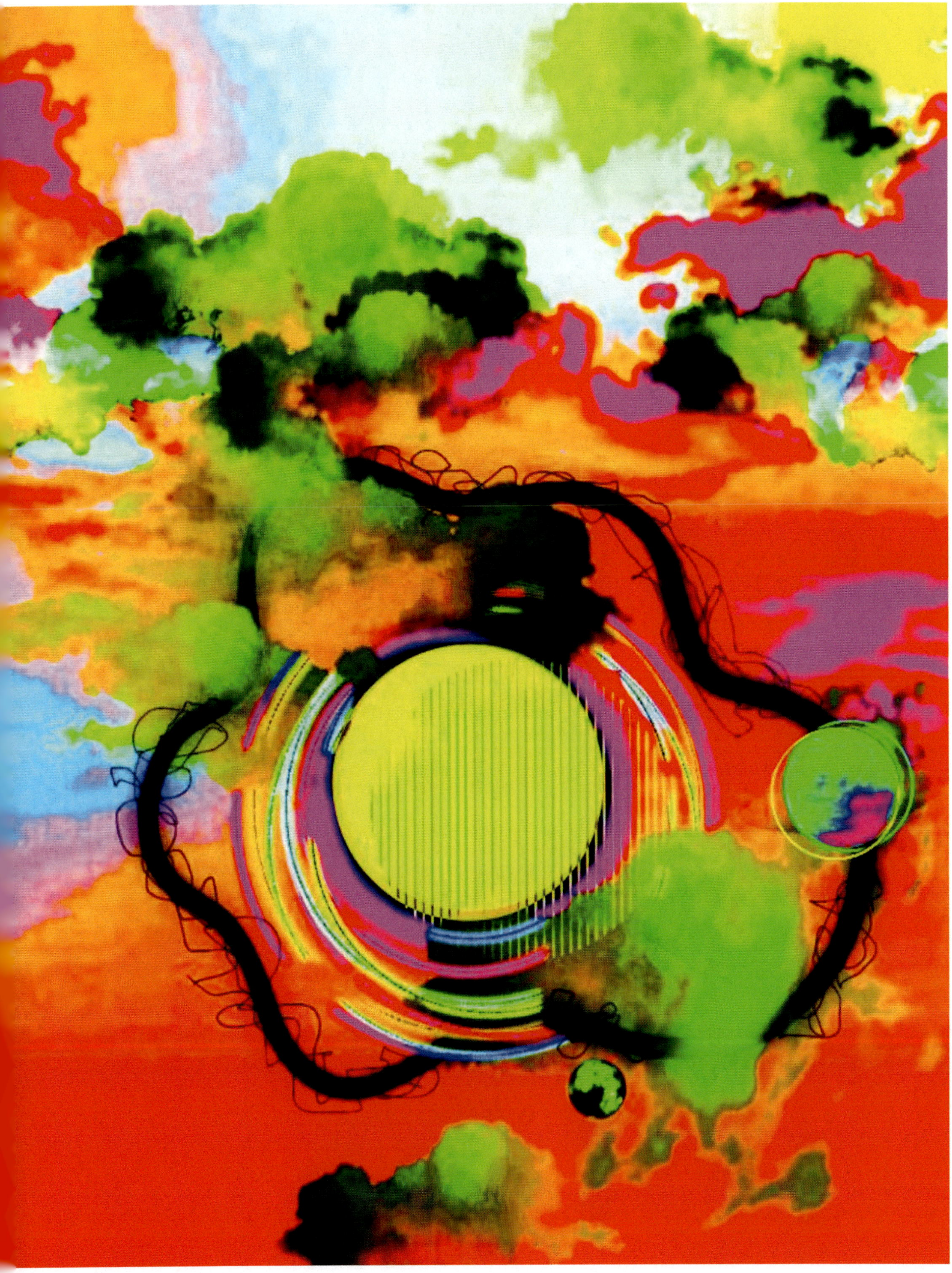

Moddgue Rocks

PREP TIME: 1 hour // COOK TIME: 20 minutes // YIELD: 6-8 servings

Onion & Apricot Biscuits
Sage Gravy

INGREDIENTS

1 Deo rocks recipe
1 Moddgue podge recipe
1 bunch fresh sage, diced
Ground Paprika
1 cup smoked gouda, grated

CREATION

1. Prepare deo rocks recipe.
2. Prepare moddgue podge recipe while deo rocks are baking.
3. Prepare Topping:
a. Slice fresh sage
b. Once plated, place deo rocks on plate, cover with a little gouda then cover top with moddgue podge recipe. Garnish with paprika and sage.
c. Serve hot.

Mud Pies

PREP TIME: 5 minutes // COOK TIME: 15 minutes // YIELD: 16 Servings

INGREDIENTS

3 cups flour
8 teaspoons baking powder
2 teaspoons salt
1 ½ cup buttermilk
1 ½ cups milk
2 eggs
7 tablespoons butter, melted
4 tablespoons sugar
2 teaspoons vanilla

Lemon Chamomile
Prepare as said, add one bag of chamomile tea
Zest of lemon

Avocado vanilla
Prepare as said, add one avocado, mashed
Add 1 more teaspoon vanilla
Add ½ cup milk

Rosemary maple
Prepare as said, add 3 teaspoons fresh rosemary, diced finely

CREATION

a. Prepare cast iron pan or griddle, heat on medium, so its ready when batter is done.
b. In large mixing bowl, add all dry ingredients, mix well.
c. Add liquid ingredients and mix well until creamy.
d. Using a scoop, (I use a cookie scoop, so they are all even), scoop about 2 inches apart from one another, onto a buttered surface. Cook until lightly golden, then flip, cook until other side is golden.
e. Serve hot with Topcoat, or desired syrup.

Rosemary Maple
Avocado Vanilla
&
Lemon Chamomille
Pancakes

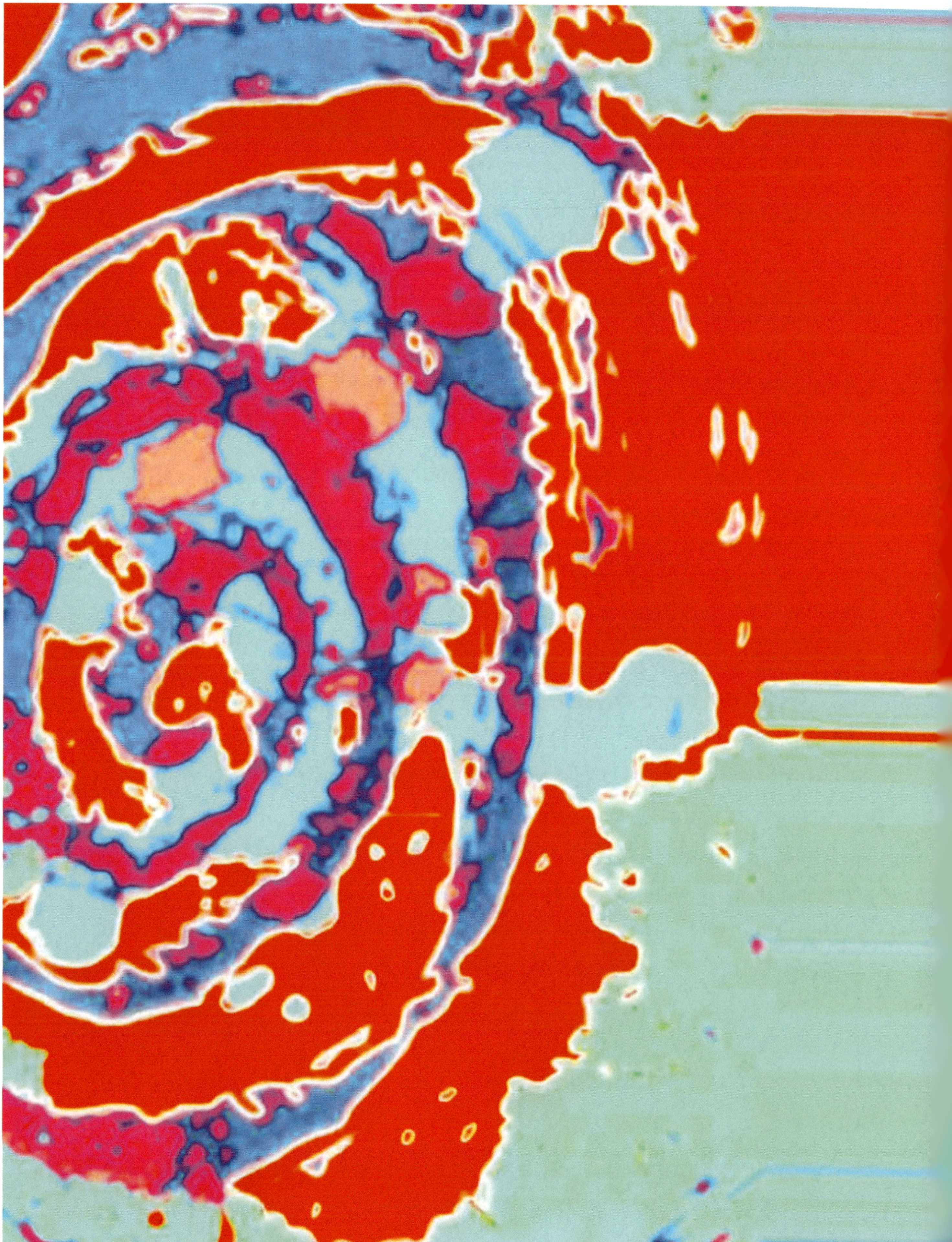

Rolled Canvas

PREP TIME: 10 minutes // COOK TIME: 20 minutes // YIELD: 16-20 crepes

INGREDIENTS

8 eggs
4 cups milk, warm
8 tablespoons butter, melted
2 tablespoons sugar
4 teaspoons vanilla
1 teaspoon salt,
3 cups flour, sifted

Sweet Potato Crepes:
Add 1 cup mashed sweet potato to mixture
Add 2 teaspoons finely diced thyme
Add ¼ cup milk

Preparing marshmallow topping:
melt 2 tablespoons butter, 2 cups marshmallows over medium heat until melted and mixed well, drizzle over top of sweet potato crepes.

Red chili crepes:
Add 1 teaspoon ground red chili pepper to mixture.
Melt 2 baking bars of chocolate or white chocolate add ½ teaspoon ground red chili pepper to melted chocolate, drizzle over top.

Zucchini Cake Crepes:
Add 1 cup grated zucchini to mixture
Add 1 teaspoon cinnamon to mixture

CREATION

a. Heat milk up just until warm, do not over-heat it, or it will cook the eggs and you don't want that.

b. Melt butter, Add to large mixing bowl, add milk, mix well. Make sure mixture is warm, not hot. Then add eggs in, whisk well.

c. Add sugar, vanilla and salt; mix well.

d. add sifted flour, one cup at a time, whisking mixture so it remains creamy and not lumpy.

e. Once all flour has been added... heat desired pan for making crepes. Not everyone will have a crepe pan in their cabinet, I prefer using a cast iron, it cooks fast.

f. Using ladle, pour one full ladle of batter onto hot pan, spread until thin, do this step fast as it cooks fast.

g. Cook until side up looks cooked as well, usually 1-2 minutes. Flip, cook other side for 30 seconds.

h. Serve hot.

Sweet Potato & Thyme
Red Chili
Zucchini Cake Crepes

Quick Sand

PREP TIME: 5-10 minutes // COOK TIME: 5-10 minutes // YIELD: 6 servings

Coffee BrownSugar Fig & Plum Oatmeal

INGREDIENTS

3 cups oats

3 ½ cups of water

1 ½ teaspoons salt

1 cup brown sugar

1 cup fresh fig, sliced

1 cup fresh plum, sliced

1 tablespoon fresh ground coffee

1 tablespoon brown sugar

¼ cup butter

CREATION

a. Bring water and salt in medium saucepan to boil, over medium heat.

b. Once water has came to a boil. Add in oats. Cook, stirring constantly about 1-2 minutes. Remove from heat.

c. Add butter, stir to melt butter in oats.

d. Add brown sugar, mix well.

e. Scoop out oatmeal into individual bowls.

f. Add sliced fig and plums to top of oatmeal.

g. In small bowl, mix coffee grounds and brown sugar, mix well.

h. Sprinkle coffee and brown sugar over top of oatmeal.

i. Serve hot.

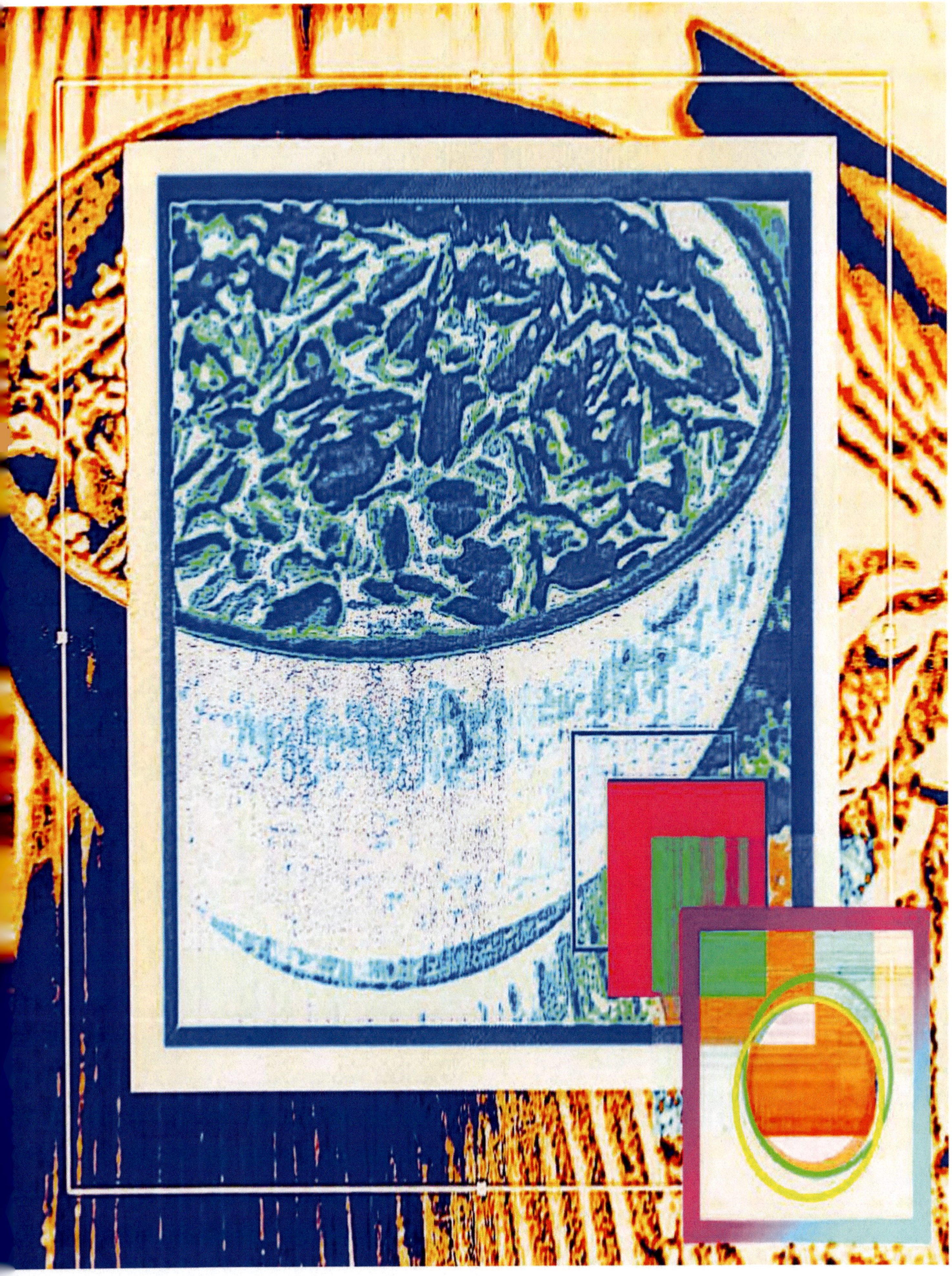

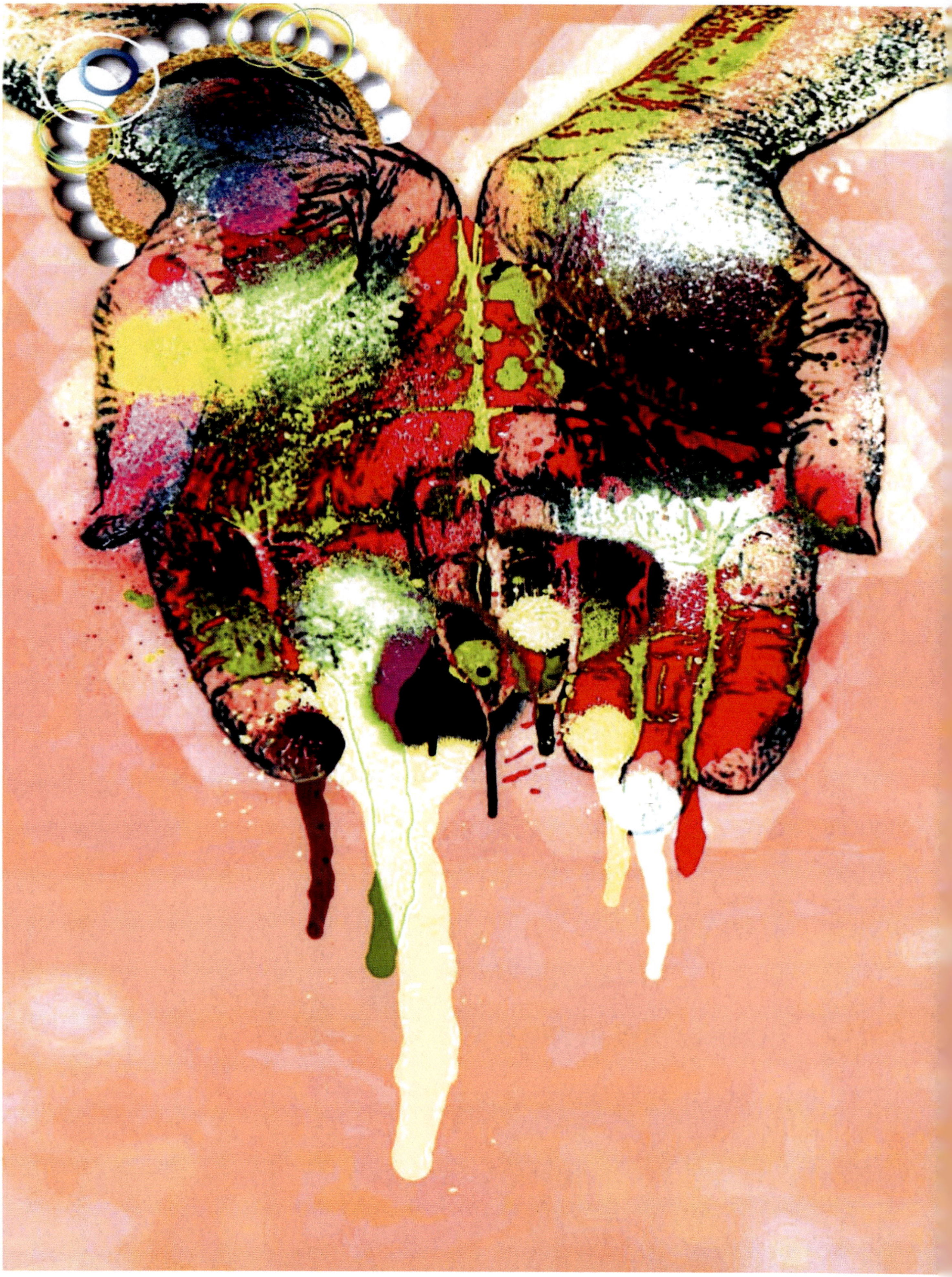

Kristine's Masterpiece

PREP TIME: 15 minutes // COOK TIME: 25 minutes // YIELD: 6-8 Servings

---

INGREDIENTS

2 Cups white rice

1-pound chicken tenders or chicken breasts, large dice

1 yellow onion, diced

16 oz sour cream

3 tablespoons clarified butter

1 tablespoon flour

2 chicken bouillon cubes

3-4 teaspoons ground paprika

Zest of one orange

1 teaspoon pepper

2 tablespoons water

Diced chives for top

Orange & Paprika Chicken

CREATION

1. Prepare Rice:

a. In medium saucepan. Prepare two cups of rice. Add two cups of rice to pan, add 3 ½ cups of water, cover and cook over medium heat until water boils. Reduce heat and let simmer, keeping lid on pan, to keep the steam inside. Until rice is light and fluffy. While your rice cooks….

2. Prepare Orange chicken Sauce:

a. In large skillet, add chicken and onions until chicken is fully cooked, over medium heat.

b. Remove chicken from skillet and set aside.

c. Add butter and melt.

d. Add flour to make a roux, cook for 2-3 minutes.

e. Add chicken bouillon cubes, paprika and 2 tablespoons water. Mix well.

e. Add chicken, mix well.

f. Add sour cream, mix. Cook until sour cream is hot.

g. Add orange zest and pepper.

h. Serve sauce over rice. Add diced chives to top, serve hot.

Pansta

PREP TIME: 10 minutes // COOK TIME: 30 minutes // YIELD: 6-8 servings

INGREDIENTS

1 Pigment recipe
16 oz Angel hair pasta
16 oz fresh mozzarella, sliced

Pancetta & Basil Pasta

CREATION

1. Prepare Pasta:

a. In large pot, fill with water and 1 teaspoon salt. Bring to a boil.

b. Add pasta and cook until aldente.

c. While pasta cooks, prepare Pigment recipe.

2. Prepare Pigment:

3. Prepare Pansta:

a. When pasta is cooked to aldente, strain.

b. Slice fresh mozzarella in ¼ thick slices, place two slices on plate.

c. Place pasta serving over fresh mozzarella.

d. Pour desired amount of sauce over pasta.

Dew Platable Nara

PREP TIME: 10 minutes // COOK TIME: 25 minutes // YIELD: 6-8 servings

INGREDIENTS

1-pound penne pasta
1 honey dew melon, diced
8oz fresh mozzarella
1-pound fresh prosciutto, diced
3 cups fresh basil
1 ½ teaspoons salt
1 ½ teaspoons pepper
2 egg yolks
1 garlic clove, minced
1 shallot, diced
3 tablespoons olive oil

Handwritten notes: Carbonara Style Pasta / ~~Honey~~ Dew Melon / Crispy Prcuitto

CREATION

1. Prepare pasta:
a. In large pot, add a little salt. Bring to a boil over medium heat.
b. While water is heating up, prepare the rest.
c. Once water has come to a boil, add pasta. Cook until pasta is aldente.
d. Strain water from pasta, set aside.

2. Prepare the rest:
a. In large skillet, heat over medium heat.
b. Add diced prosciutto, cook until lightly crispy.
c. Add garlic, and shallots, honey dew melon. Mix.
d. Once melon is hot, add pasta. Reduce heat to low.
e. Add salt, pepper, egg yolks, mix well.
f. Add fresh basil, without stems. Stir around to mix in basil and cook only until basil wilts a little.
g. Remove from heat. Dice fresh mozzarella.
h. Plate the pasta, add dice fresh mozzarella to top. Serve hot.

Artistic Plateau

PREP TIME: 10 minutes // COOK TIME: 15 minutes // YIELD: 6-8 servings

INGREDIENTS

1 Plateau Recipe or pizza dough of choice
2-3 bananas, sliced
2 cup fresh basil, diced
Yellow curry powder
2 cups smoked cheeses, parmesean, asiago and gouda, grated
Marinara of choice, or use Pigment recipe)
Add diced ham (optional)

CREATION

1. Prepare pizza dough and marinara:
2. Prepare pizza:
a. Slice and dice bananas and basil, grate cheese. Set aside.
b. Place pizza dough on parchment lined baking sheet. Poke holes in doughs surface.
c. Preheat oven to 425*F.
d. Cover dough with layer of marinara or pigment recipe.
e. Add grated cheeses to cover entire surface.
f. Add sliced bananas to cover entire surface, sprinkle basil over top.
g. Add ham if you choose.
h. Sprinkle yellow curry powder over entire pizza, generously.
i. Bake for 10-15 minutes until dough is golden and cheese is completely melted. Remove from oven.
j. Let cool a few minutes before cutting and serving.

Banana Curry Pizza

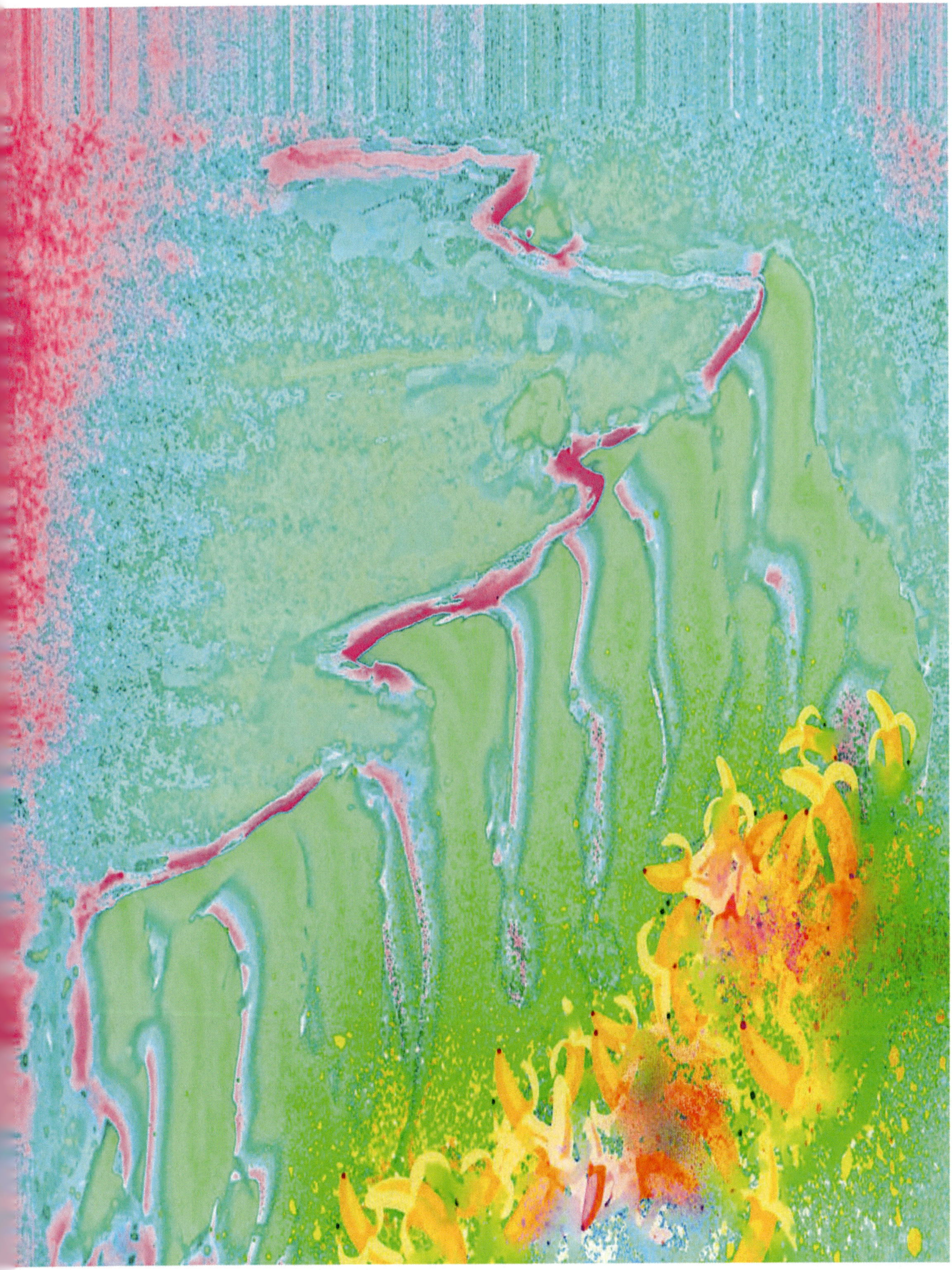

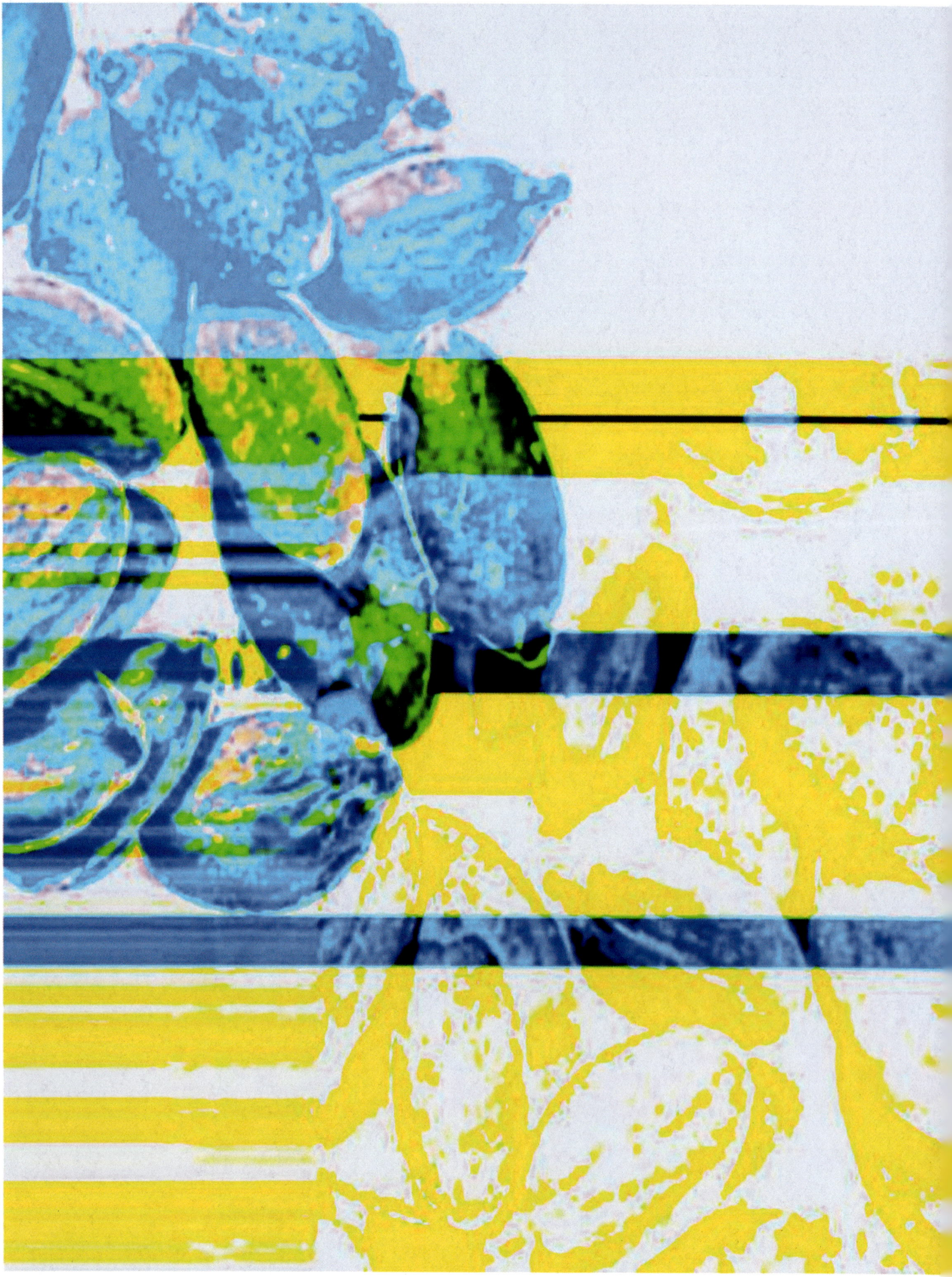

Mossed Ocean & Tart Seeds

PREP TIME: 10 minutes // COOK TIME: 25 minutes // YIELD: 6-8 servings

INGREDIENTS

6 fresh cod fillets, thick fillets work best
1 shallot, diced
½ teaspoon salt
½ teaspoon white pepper
2 tablespoons olive oil.
Zest from 1 lemon
1 Melted bricks recipe
1 Brinded harvest recipe

Roasted Cod
Matcha Buerre Blanc
Pickled Lentils

CREATION

1. Prepare Brined harvest recipe:

a. Preparing brined harvest ahead of time, makes it easier, considering the brinded portion takes a little time.

2. Prepare cod:

a. Preheat oven to 400*F

b. Pat the cod fillets with paper towel to remove any excess liquid.

c. Sprinkle the salt and pepper over top of each cod fillets.

d. Pour olive in baking pan, add fillets to baking pan. Sprinkle lemon zest to tops of fillets.

e. Cook in oven for about 10-20 minutes, depending on thickness of fillets. Cook until the fish begins to flake with a fork. While cod roasts in oven......

3. Prepare Melted bricks recipe:

a. Prepare melted bricks recipe.

4. Prepare final step:

a. Plate the fish on plate, with brined harvest as a side. Pour desired amount of melted brick recipe over fish.

Forest & Bulbs

Thyme & Tangerine Lamb

PREP TIME: 15 minutes // COOK TIME: 30 minutes // YIELD: 6 Servings

INGREDIENTS

6 fresh lamb chops
2 cups fresh pearl onions, whole
2 parsnips, diced
½ cup red wine vinegar
4 tablespoons fresh thyme, diced
Zest from 3 tangerines
2 tablespoons honey
1 teaspoon salt
1 teaspoon pepper
½ cup beef stock
2 tablespoons butter, cubes
2 tablespoons clarified butter or extra virgin coconut oil

CREATION

a. In large skillet, preferably cast iron, heat over medium-high heat, add oil.

b. Salt and pepper lamb chops on both sides. Add to hot skillet. Cook for 1-2 minutes on both sides to brown.

b. Preheat oven to 400*F

c. Add pearl onions, parsnips, red wine vinegar, beef stock, thyme and honey until boils.

d. Remove from heat, Add tangerine zest and drizzle honey over top. Add butter cubes to top of each chop. Cover and place in oven for 20 minutes.

e. Remove from oven and plate. Serve hot.

European Mud Pies

PREP TIME: 10 minutes // COOK TIME: 25 minutes // YIELD: 6 Servings

INGREDIENTS

2-pounds ground pork
2 garlic cloves, minced
1 1/2 teaspoons oregano
1 teaspoon red chili powder
2 teaspoons paprika
1 teaspoon salt
1 teaspoon pepper
8 oz of sun-dried tomatoes
4 oz tomato paste
8 oz sour cream
1 yellow onion, diced
Hamburger buns of choice (potato or sweet Hawaiian is best)
2 tablespoons clarified butter or extra virgin coconut oil

CREATION

a. In large skillet, add oil to pan, heat over medium.

b. Add ground pork, cook until done.

c. Add onions and garlic. Mix: cook until onions are soft.

d. Add tomato paste, cook until tomato paste turns deeper in color.

e. Add sun dried tomatoes, mix well.

f. Add salt, pepper, paprika, oregano and red chili powder; cook for 5 minutes.

g. Add sour cream; cook until sour cream is hot and well mixed.

h. Remove from heat, serve in hamburger buns, serve hot.

Swedish Stroganoff Sloppy Joes

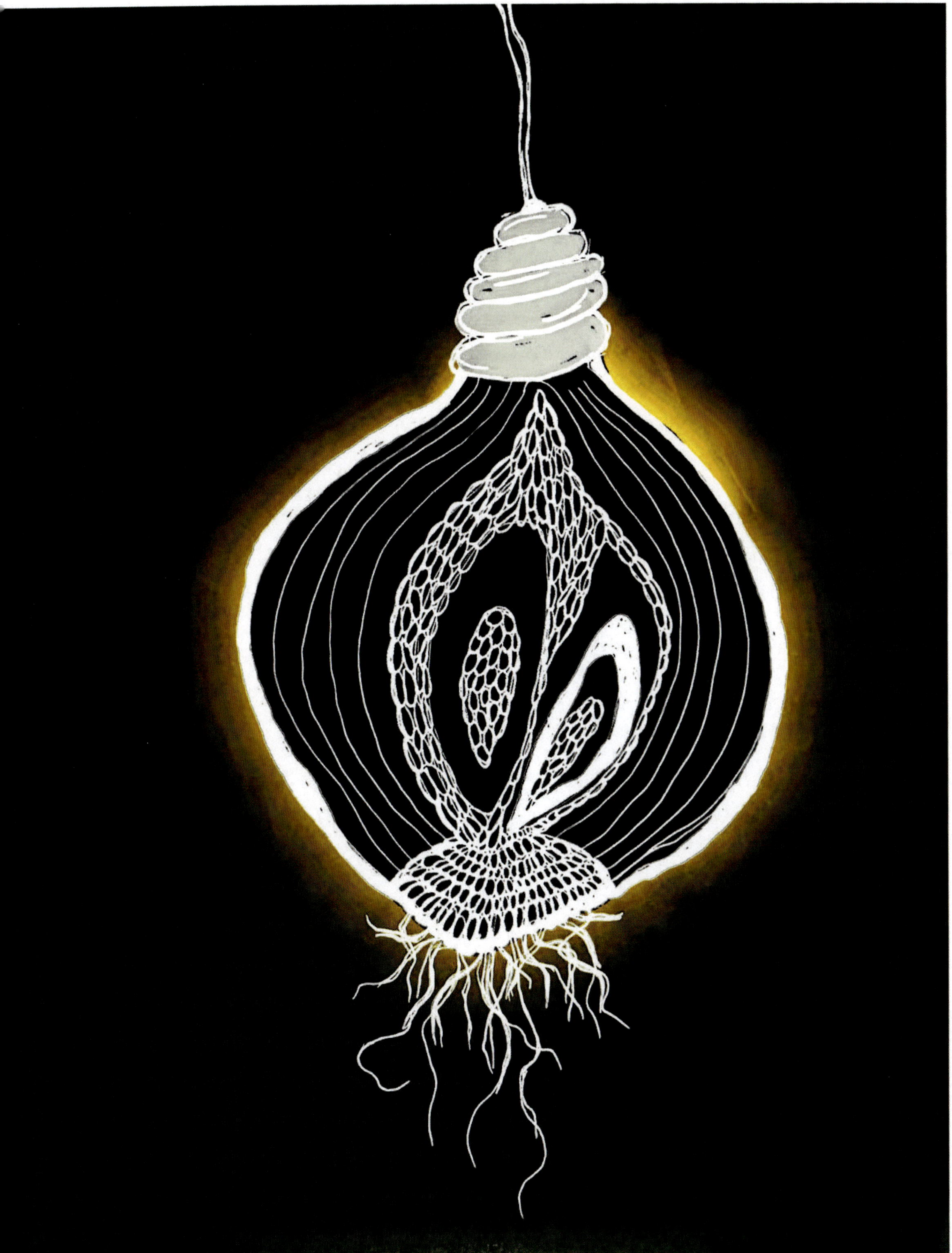

75

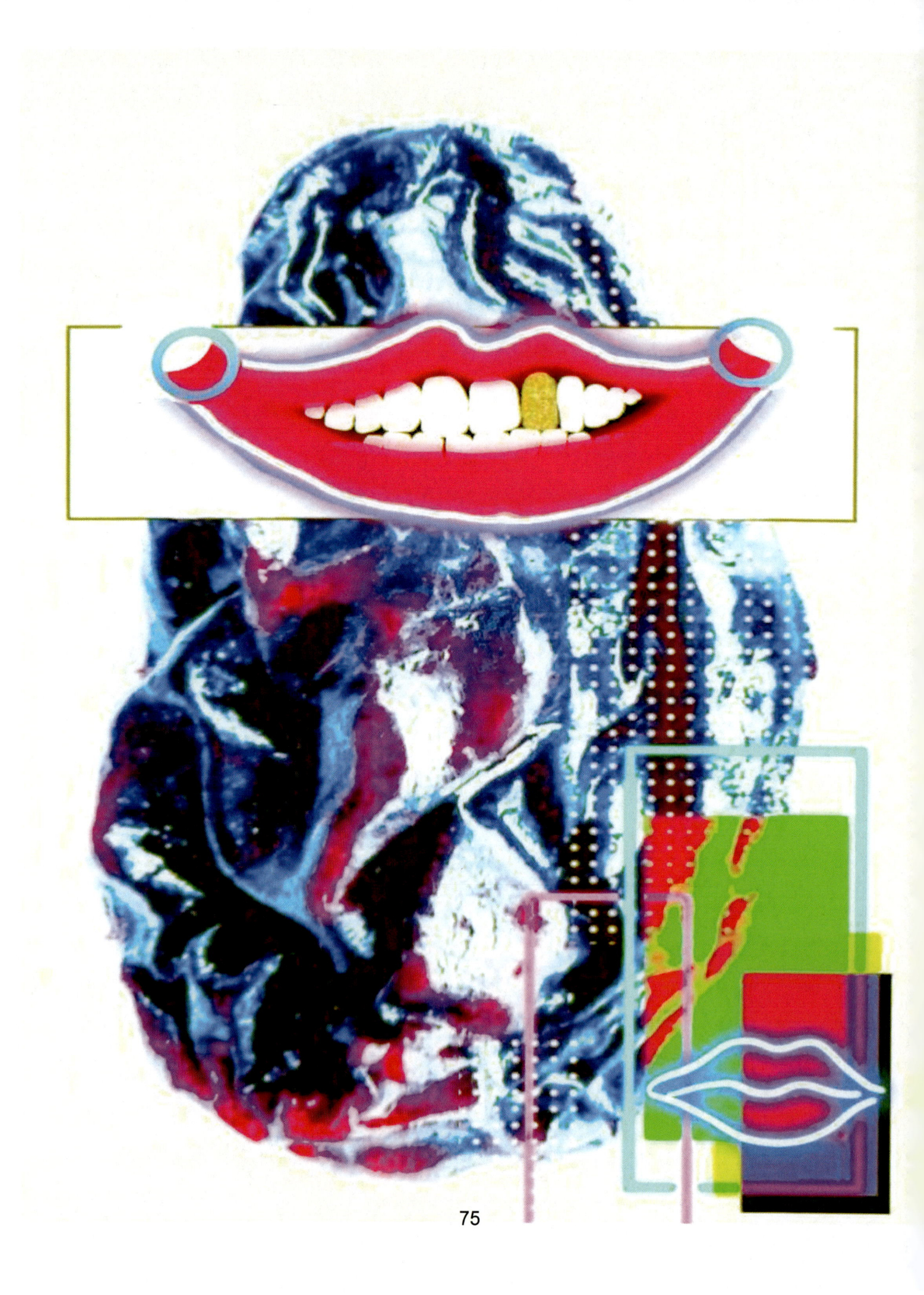

Sir Fermented

Red Wine & Sweet Peppers Pasta

PREP TIME: 10 minutes // COOK TIME: 25 minutes // YIELD: 6-8 servings

INGREDIENTS

1-pound bowtie pasta

1 cup sweet peppers, sliced

1 shallot, sliced

1 cup dry red wine

1 cup sweet red wine

4 tablespoons balsamic vinegar

3 tablespoons fresh thyme, diced

2 tablespoon clarified butter

1 teaspoon salt

1 teaspoon pepper

1 clove garlic, minced

1 cup fresh parmesan cheese, shredded

CREATION

1. **Prepare pasta:**

a. In large pot, add a little salt. Bring to a boil over medium heat.

b. While water is heating up, prepare sauce.

c. Once water has come to a boil, add pasta. Cook until pasta is aldente. Strain and set aside.

2. **Prepare red wine sauce:**

a. In medium saucepan, pour wine in, reduce over medium heat until wine becomes a bit thicker in texture.

b. Remove from pan, using same pan, add shallot, garlic, peppers, cook until soft.

c. Add balsamic vinegar, red wine. Mix well. Leaving on heat, on low.

d. Add fresh thyme, diced.

e. Add salt and pepper. Mix. Remove from heat.

d. Add butter, while sauce is hot. Stir in pasta; ensuring all pasta is coated.

e. Serve hot, sprinkle fresh parmesan cheese over top.

Painted Sunset

PREP TIME: 15 minutes // COOK TIME: 25 minutes // YIELD: 6-8 Servings

INGREDIENTS

16-18 oz fresh blueberries
4 anaheim peppers, diced
1 pork tenderloin (1 pound or more)
2 cups green cabbage, sliced
Zest from 2 limes
Juice from one lime
2 teaspoons salt
2 teaspoons pepper
2 garlic cloves, minced
½ teaspoon ground cumin
1 Picant-so recipe
1 circular canvas recipe

INGREDIENTS FOR WHITE CHOCOLATE DRIZZLE

3- Baking white chocolate bars
½ teaspoon red chili powder 1 tablespoon heavy cream

CREATION

1. **Prepare Circular canvas recipe:**
a. Works best if you make ahead of time, tortillas are a little time consuming. Wrap up and set aside.

2. **Prepare Picant-so Recipe:**
a. Prepare peach picant-so recipe and cool.
b. Slice cabbage and place in small bowl, add lime juice to cabbage and toss, set aside.

3. **Prepare pork:**
a. In large saucepan, pot or crock-pot, put pork tenderloin in it, with a couple table spoons of water. Ensure lid is on as you want to creation steam in the pot/pan to allow the tenderloin to cook and stay moist.
b. Cook tenderloin until tenderloin shreds.
c. In large skillet, add onions, garlic and diced anaheim peppers; cook until onions are softer.
d. Add blueberries, cook until blueberries break down, but still have some shape to them.
e. Add salt, pepper, cumin and zest of 2 limes. Mix.
f. Shred pork and add pork to blueberry mix.
g. Reduce heat and let mixture simmer while you prepare white chocolate drizzle.

4. **Prepare white chocolate drizzle:**
a. In small saucepan, add heavy cream, heat until hot.
b. Break white chocolate into pieces and add to heavy cream.
c. Cook over low-medium heat until chocolate is completely melted and smooth in texture.
d. Add chili powder. Remove from heat.

5. **Prepare final dish:**
a. On plate, place tortilla, pork mixture, add peach salsa, a little cabbage and drizzle with white chocolate sauce. Serve hot.

LUEBER
RY

Coastal Twisters

PREP TIME: 15 minutes // COOK TIME: 25 minutes // YIELD: 6-8 servings

Tuna Dill Lemon Zest Pasta

INGREDIENTS

1-pound tricolor fusilli twist pasta
3 teaspoons fresh dill
Zest of 3 lemons
2 fresh tuna fillets
1/3 cup heavy cream
4 tablespoons clarified butter
2 tablespoons olive oil
1 shallot, diced
2 parsnips, diced
1 teaspoon salt
1 teaspoon white pepper

CREATION

1. Prepare tuna:

a. Preheat oven to 400*F.

b. In mixing bowl, add shallot, parsnip, olive oil. Set aside.

c. Pat dry fresh tuna fillets to remove excess liquid.

d. Place tuna fillets in baking pan, pour olive oil mixture over tuna.

e. Put in oven and bake until tuna begins to flake with fork. Then remove from oven.

f. While tuna cooks, prepare pasta.

2. Prepare pasta:

a. In large pot, add a little salt. Bring to a boil over medium heat.

b. While water is heating up, prepare sauce.

c. Once water has come to a boil, add pasta. Cook until pasta is aldente. Strain and set aside.

3. Prepare Sauce

a. In large skillet, add butter, over medium heat. Melt butter.

b. Add tuna fillets, break apart tuna so its 'shredded'. Add shallots and parsnips and excess olive oil from baking pan into the skillet.

c. Add heavy cream mix well. Reduce heat.

d. Add lemon zest, dill, mix well.

e. Add pasta when sauce is hot. Turn heat off.

f. Add salt and pepper. Mix. Serve hot.

Scarlet River Beads

PREP TIME: 15 minutes // COOK TIME: 25 minutes // YIELD: 6-8 servings

Macaroni & Cheese
White Cheddar
Trout Roe

INGREDIENTS

1-pound macaroni
1 cup sundried tomatoes
1 bunch chives, diced
4 cups sharp white cheddar cheese, shredded
1 shallot, diced
3 cups heavy cream
1 teaspoon red chili powder
½ teaspoon salt
1 teaspoon white pepper
½ cup butter
Trout roe for top (about 1 teaspoon per serving)

CREATION

1. **Prepare macaroni:**
a. In large pot, add a little salt. Bring to a boil over medium heat.
b. While water is heating up, prepare sauce.
c. Once water has come to a boil, add pasta. Cook until pasta is aldente. Strain and set aside.

2. **Prepare cheese sauce:**
a. In large saucepan, melt butter over medium heat.
b. Add shallot and sundried tomatoes, cook until shallots are soft.
c. Add heavy cream, heat until hot.
d. Add cheese and whisk until melted.
e. Add red chili powder, salt and pepper. Remove from heat.
f. Add macaroni, mix so that the macaroni is completed covered in cheese sauce.
g. After plating macaroni with cheese sauce, top with trout roe and chives. Serve hot.

SPONGE BOARDS

INGREDIENTS

1 (8 ounce) package of cream cheese

⅓ cup mayonnaise

¼ cup sour cream

1 minced clove of garlic

¼ cup minced shallot ¼ cup shave,

1 cup artichoke hearts 1 cup fresh spinach, without stems

1 teaspoon shaved black truffle

a. In medium-large sauce pan, add white wine, minced garlic and minced shallots. Cook 1-2 minutes on medium heat.

b. Add cream cheese, sour cream and mayonnaise, cook on medium heat, stirring constantly while cooking, to prevent mixture from burning, until mixture is creamy in texture.

c. Add artichoke hearts and parmesan cheese, mix in and cook over heat until cheese has melted.

d. Low heat, add fresh spinach, cook until spinach is... Usually

f. Serve hot.

INGREDIENTS

Citrus Felt

Dash of Salt & Pepper

c. Add diced green onion to avocado and mix well.

d. Zest 2 lemons, add zest to avocado mixture, mix well.

e. Dice red grapes, add to mixture, combine until mixed.

f. Add salt and pepper, to taste.

g. Spread over toast of choice.

Empty Stage *Pie Dough*

PREP TIME: 15 minutes // COOK TIME: 0 minutes // YIELD: 8-10 Servings

INGREDIENTS

2 cups flour

¾ tablespoon sugar

1 teaspoon salt

¾ -1 cup cold butter, cubed

1 vanilla bean, scraped

2 tablespoons fresh sage, diced

2 teaspoons apple cider vinegar

¼-1/2 cup ice water

CREATION

a. In large bowl, mix all dry ingredients.

b. Add cold butter, using a metal fork or pastry cutter, cut butter into flour mixture.

c. Add vanilla and sage. Mix.

d. Add in vinegar and ice water, using wooden spoon mix together until it becomes more difficult to use a spoon.

e. Using hands, knead dough until dough holds together and is no longer loose.

f. Divide dough in half. Roll each piece into a ball and wrap with plastic wrap. Place in refrigerator to cool. Minimum 1 hour.

g. When ready to use, remove from refrigerator and roll out dough on lightly floured surface, using rolling pin (also lightly floured).

h. Once rolled to desired size, place in baking pie dish and press against sides.

i. To bake: Preheat oven to 375*F. Bake until pie crust is lightly golden in color.

Citrus Sponge Branch

PREP TIME: 15 minutes // COOK TIME: 60 minutes // YIELD: 12 servings

INGREDIENTS

2 cups flour
1 teaspoon baking soda
½ teaspoon baking powder
Pinch of salt
Zest of 3 lemons
½ cup butter
1 cup sugar
½ cup lemon juice
½ cup milk
3 eggs
1 teaspoon anise extract
1 vanilla bean paste

Lemon & Anise Quick Bread

CREATION

a. Preheat oven 350*F

b. in large mixing bowl, add flour, baking powder, baking soda, salt. Mix together, set aside.

c. in small mixing bowl, add sugar and lemon zest, mix.

d. in large, separate mixing bowl, whisk eggs and butter until creamy.

e. Add sugar and lemon zest mixture to eggs, continue to whisk until light and creamy.

f. Add lemon juice, this will cause a little separation or curdling of the batter (because of the acidity, its ok!) mix until combined.

g. Add flour mixture a little at a time, until well combined.

h. Add in anise extract and vanilla bean paste, mix.

i. pour into well-greased and floured baking pan, bake for 60 minutes or until golden and toothpick inserted comes out clean.

j. Cool completely before eating.

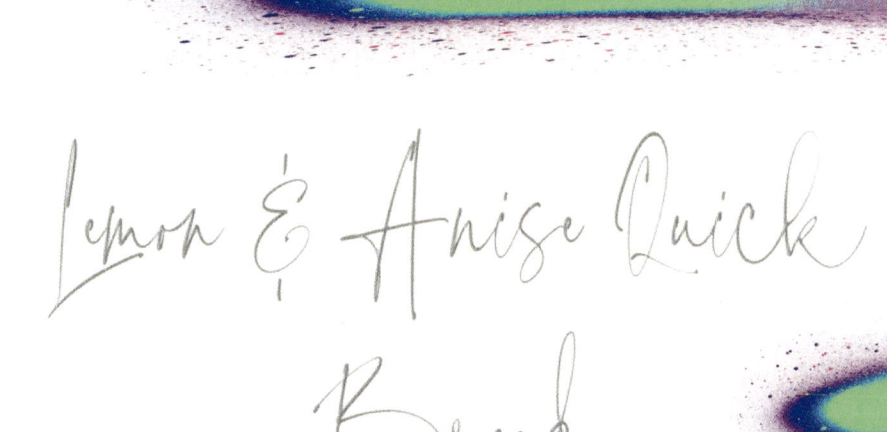

Skipped Sidewalk Knots

PREP TIME: 20 minutes // COOK TIME: 20-25 minutes // YIELD: 12 Servings

INGREDIENTS

1 stick butter, unsalted
1 1/2 cup warm water
7 tablespoon sugar
4 ½ teaspoons active dry yeast
1 ½ teaspoons salt
½ cup powdered milk
6 cups flour
3 tablespoons rye seeds
Coarse sugar for top

INGREDIENTS FOR FILLING

1 1/2 sticks unsalted butter
½ cup sugar
2 tablespoons ground cinnamon
2 tablespoons ground cardamom

INGREDIENTS FOR EGG WASH

1 large egg
1 tablespoon milk

Cardamom Rolls

CREATION

1. **Prepare dough:**
a. In a large mixing bowl, add warm water, melted butter and sugar, mix well.
b. Sprinkle yeast over the mixture and set aside, until yeast dissolves and creates a foam texture in mixture.
c. Add eggs, milk powder, salt and rye seeds; mix together. d. Add 6 cups of the flour, one cup at a time, stirring continuously, until each cup of flour is mixed in, do this for each cup of flour.
e. Remove dough from bowl and place onto a lightly floured surface.
f. Knead dough for 8-10 minutes, until the dough is smooth and elastic in texture. Make sure dough is not sticky but not dried out either. Do not add too much flour when kneading. But just enough to prevent it from sticking or drying out.
g. Shape the kneaded dough into a ball.
h. Place ball of dough in a bowl and cover with plastic wrap.
i. Let dough rise for 1 hour, until double in size.
j. While dough rises...
2. **Prepare Filling:**
a. Combine butter, sugar, cinnamon and cardamom; mix well.
b. Set aside.
3. **Return to dough:**
a. Punch the center of the risen dough.
b. Remove dough from bowl, roll into rectangle.
c. Spread filling over surface of dough. Press filling into dough.
d. Roll dough like you would with cinnamon rolls.
e. Using knife, cut slices about 1 inch thick.
f. Place each roll on parchment lined baking sheet.
g. Cover loosely with plastic wrap and let rise another hour, until it doubles in size.
h. Preheat oven to 350* F.
i. Beat egg and milk for egg wash in bowl.
j. Brush egg wash on the surface of the rolls, once risen.
k. Sprinkle coarse sugar over top of the rolls.
l. Bake rolls for 20-25 minutes, until lightly golden.

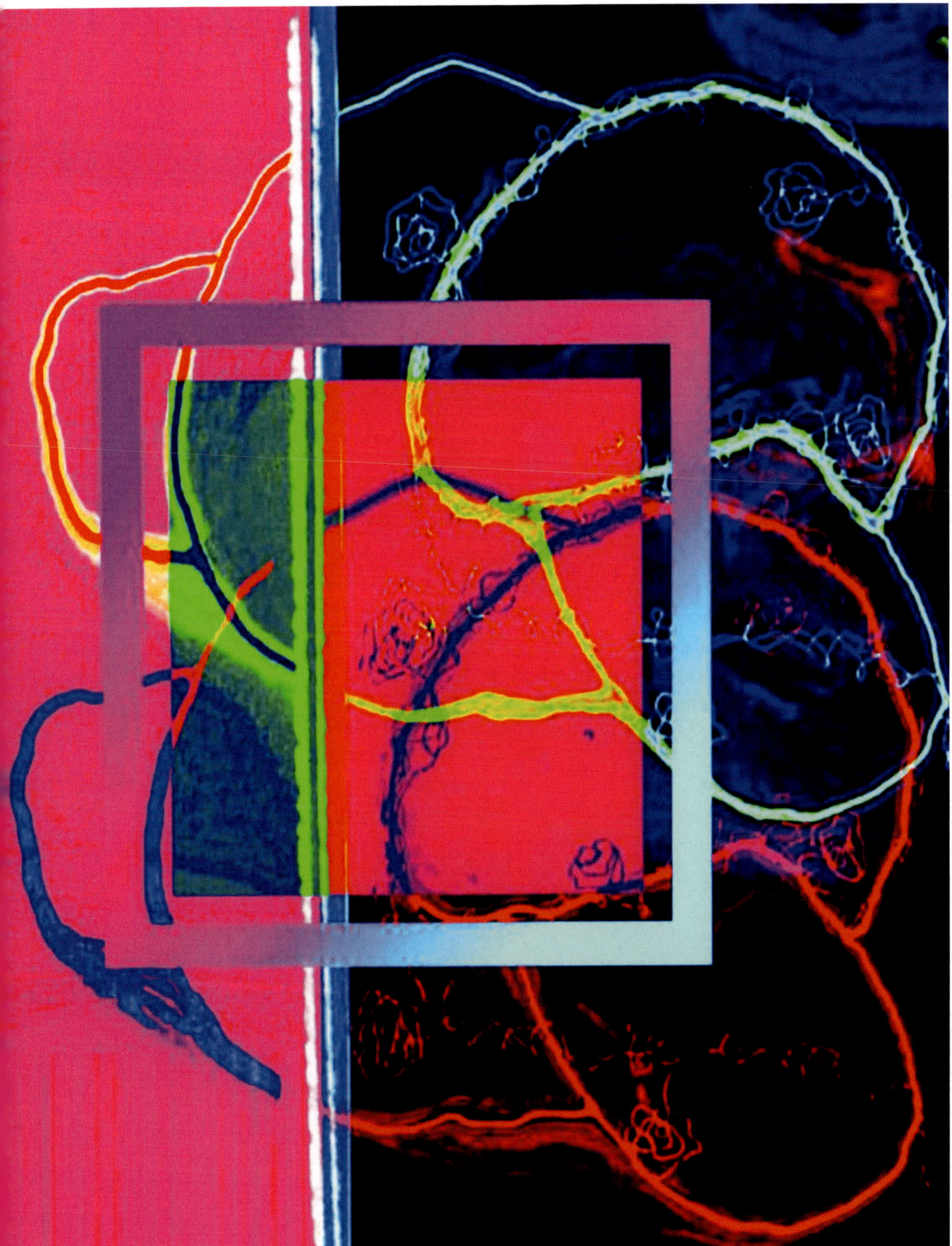

Sweet & Spicy Grounds
Anise Coffee Struesel Cake

PREP TIME: 15 minutes // COOK TIME: 20 minutes // YIELD: 12 Servings

INGREDIENTS

2 ½ Cups of flour

¾ cup light brown sugar

¾ cup sugar

1 teaspoon baking soda

1 cup (2 sticks) unsalted butter, room temp

4 eggs

1 cup sour cream

1 tablespoon vanilla extract or 2 vanilla beans

1 teaspoon anise extract or 1 teaspoon ground star anise

¾ teaspoon of salt

INGREDIENTS FOR STRUESEL

1 cup sugar

1 cup flour

½ cup of favorite coffee grounds

½ cup butter (unsalted), softened

INGREDIENTS FOR DRIZZLE TOPPING

1 cup sugar

1 tablespoon butter, melted

1 teaspoon vanilla

1 teaspoon anise

2 tablespoons heavy cream

CREATION

1. Preheat oven to 350*F
2. Prepare streusel topping.
   a. Combine flour, sugar and coffee, until well mixed.
   b. Add soft yet chilled butter, not melted to streusel mixture.
   c. Using hands to mix, creating larger chunks of mixture. Do not over mix.
   d. Set streusel mixture aside, in fridge while you make the cake.
   e. Grease baking pan with nonstick spray, butter or oil. I prefer using butter.
3. Prepare coffee cake batter:
   a. In a separate bowl from the streusel, in large bowl, whisk eggs and sugar until smooth.
   b. Add in baking soda, salt, sour cream and butter, mix until smooth and fluffy.
   c. Add vanilla and anise, stir until mixed.
   d. Add flour, mix until well mixed.
   e. Remove streusel mixture from fridge, mix with hands to make sure it breaks apart but its still chilled. spread the cake batter in greased pan.
   f. Add streusel topping over entire top of batter.
   g. Put in oven and let it bake around 40-50 minutes. Checking often. Cake is done when toothpick comes out clean and top is GBD (Golden brown delicious).
   h. Once cake is done, take out and set aside to allow to cool.
4. Prepare drizzle topping:
   a. In separate bowl, whisk heavy cream until smooth but a little thicker.
   b. Add sugar and butter. Mix well.
   c. Add vanilla and anise, until mixed.
   d. Drizzle icing over top once cake has cooled but still warm.

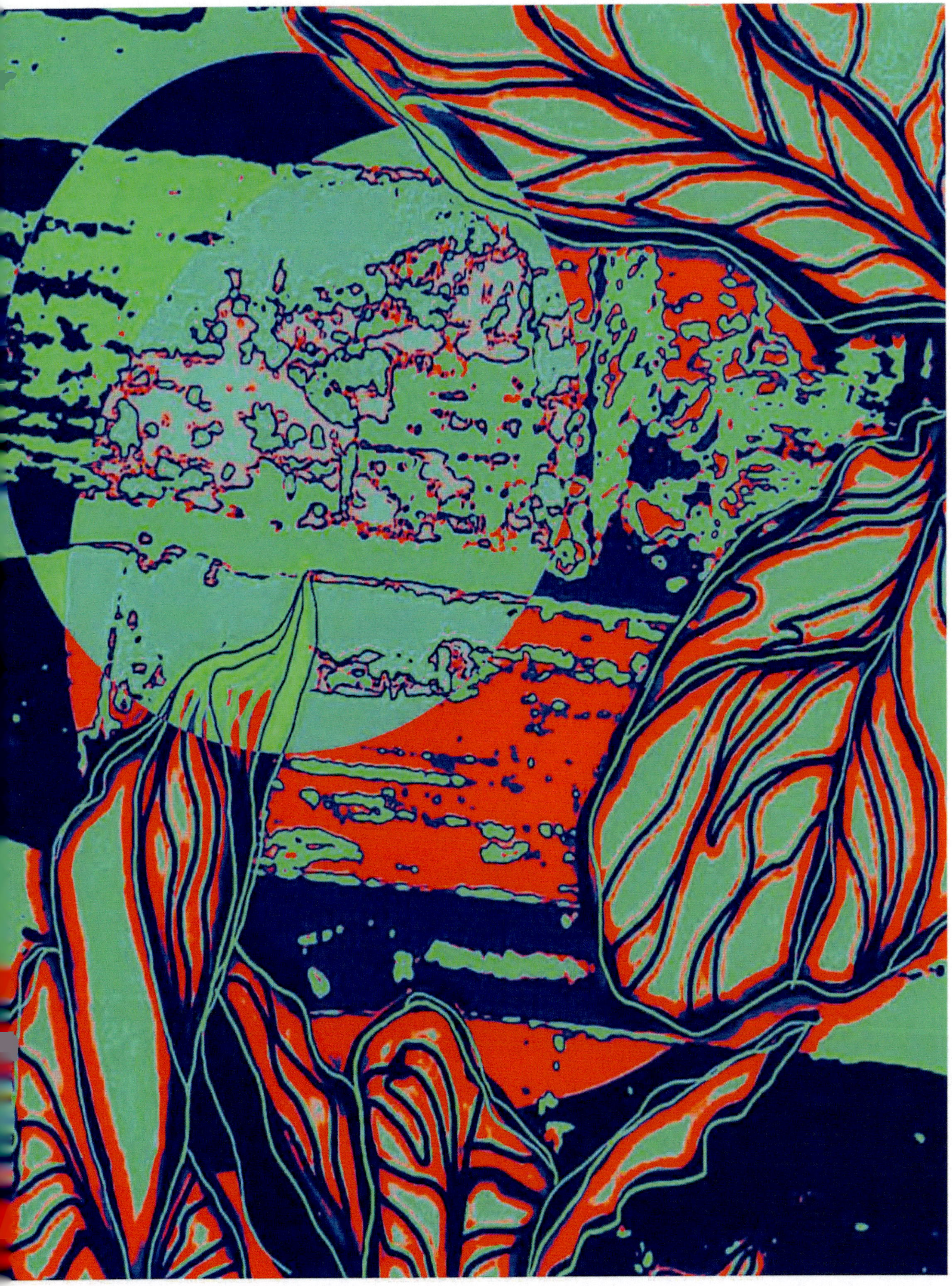

Turkish Brealight

PREP TIME: 25 minutes // COOK TIME: 30 minutes // YIELD: 12 Servings

INGREDIENTS

- 4 cups all-purpose flour
- 1 teaspoon sugar
- 1 teaspoon salt
- 1 teaspoon dry-instant yeast
- ½ cup plain Greek yogurt
- 1 cup warm water
- ½ cup warm milk
- 1 egg yolk
- 2 tablespoons softened butter
- 1 tablespoon extra virgin coconut oil
- Sesame seeds
- Nigella seeds
- Sea salt flakes

Turkish Bread Nigella Seeds

CREATION

a. In medium bowl, add warm milk, warm water, yeast and sugar to bowl, set aside until yeast bubbles and is dissolved.

b. In large bowl, add butter and oil, add salt and mix.

c. Once yeast is ready, add all ingredients into large bowl, except nigella, sesame seeds, yogurt and egg yolk.

d. Knead dough in mixer for roughly 10 minutes or by hand at least 15 minutes.

e. Turn the kneaded dough out onto a lightly floured surface and knead dough for a few more minutes.

f. Dough should be soft, if dough is firm; add a tablespoon of olive oil and knead another few minutes, until smooth.

g. After dough is kneaded and smooth, cut bread into two halves.

h. Shape out the dough on baking sheet (lined with parchment paper) using hands and fingers to shape dough into flat ovals or round, make sure dough is about ½ inch thick; evenly.

i. Mix together yolk and yogurt, brush onto dough.

j. Preheat oven to 425*F

k. Sprinkle nigella seeds and sesame seeds onto dough. Add tray of water underneath, on bottom shelf of oven, place baking sheet with bread on top shelf.

l. Bake for 30 minutes, until golden brown. Best served warm, fresh out of oven.

Circular Canvases

PREP TIME: 10 minutes // COOK TIME: 5 minutes // YIELD: 12-24 servings

INGREDIENTS

2 cups of flour
¾ teaspoon salt
¾ teaspoon baking powder
¼ cup olive oil
¾ cup warm water
½ teaspoon ground cinnamon

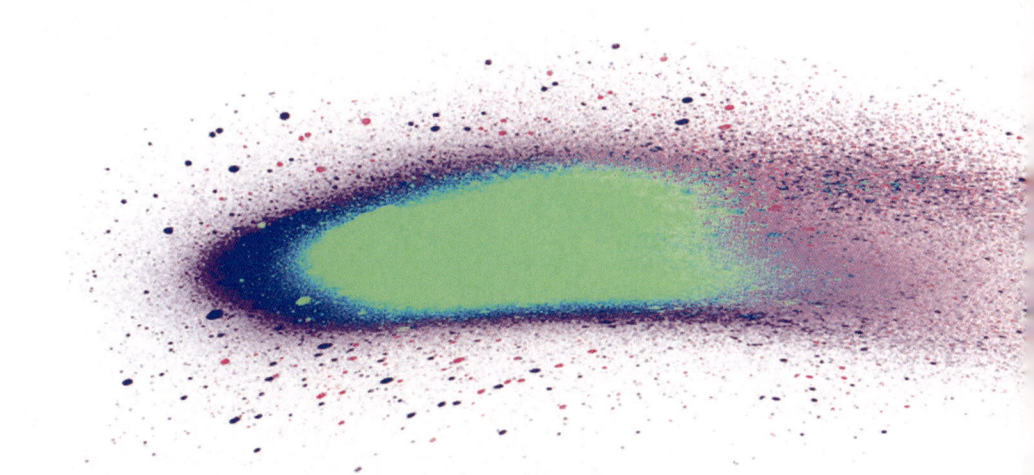

CREATION

a. In large mixing bowl, mix flour, salt, pepper, baking powder, until well combined.

b. Add olive oil, mix well.

c. Add warm water a little at a time. Mixing well, until dough forms and comes together.

d. Roll dough into small balls, keep in bowl with damp cloth over bowl to keep the dough from drying out.

e. Preheat large skillet, cast iron works best, to medium-high heat.

f. On lightly floured surface, roll out tortillas. They should be thin but not so thin that they rip.

g. Cook tortilla one side until it begins to create little bubbles, then flip and cook for just a few seconds on the other side. Tortillas cook very fast, so keep an eye on them!

h. Serve warm, can keep left over tortillas, wrap in plastic to keep air out. Can keep them for 1-2 days.

Salt, Pepper & Cinnamon Flour Tortillas

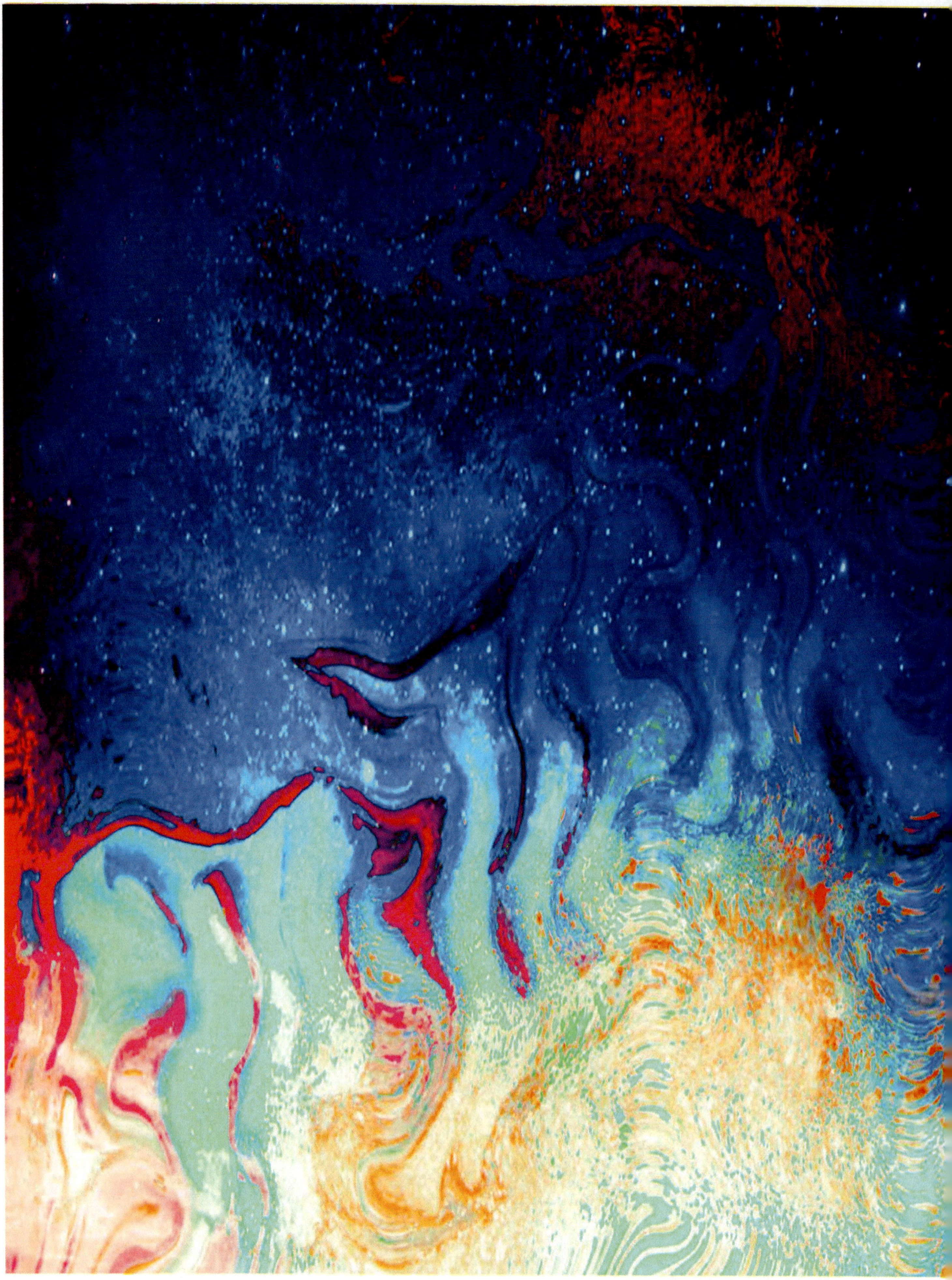

Plateau *Pizza Dough*

PREP TIME: 1 hour // COOK TIME: 15 minutes // YIELD: 12-15 inch Circle

INGREDIENTS

2 cups flour

2 teaspoons instant yeast

1 teaspoon sugar

½ teaspoon salt

2 tablespoons extra virgin coconut oil

½-3/4 cup warm water

2 tablespoons fresh basil, chopped

1 tablespoon shallots, fine diced

CREATION

a. In large bowl, mix together yeast, sugar and salt.
b. Add coconut oil and warm water to mixture and mix well.
c. Slowly but gradually add 1 cup of flour at a time until all is added and mixed. Dough will be slightly sticky, but should pull slightly away from bowl when ready for next step.
d. In separate bowl, coat inside of bowl with coconut oil, ensuring all sides are generously coated.
e. Dust hands with flour and transfer dough from mixing bowl to newly oil coated bowl, coat pizza dough with oil from bowl until dough is coated. Place plastic wrap over dough, allow dough to rise for 30 minutes.
f. Preheat oven to 425* F
g. Once dough is risen, remove dough from bowl, deflating first. Place dough on lightly floured surface. Knead dough and roll out using rolling pin (lightly floured) until desired size. (This recipe makes 12-15 inch circle.)
h. Line baking sheet with parchment paper, place dough on parchment paper.
i. Sprinkle a little coconut oil over dough coating surface. Sprinkle basil and shallots over surface of dough.
j. Poke holes through out dough, to prevent dough from gaining large bubbles.
k. Add desired toppings, like in Artistic Plateau recipe. Bake for 13-15 minutes, until dough is golden in color around edges.

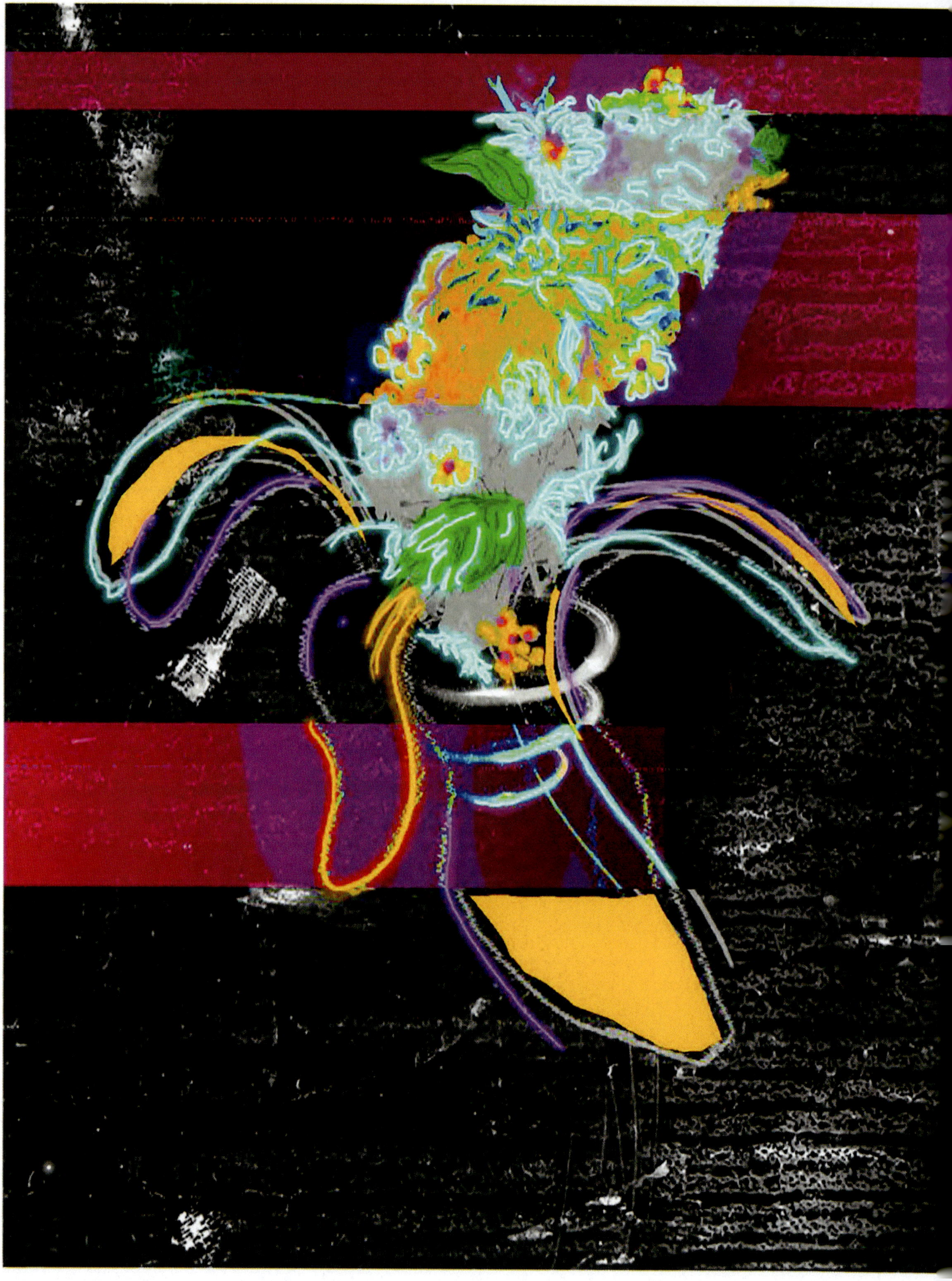

Calming Banana Board

PREP TIME: 10 minutes // COOK TIME: 20-25 minutes // YIELD: 12 servings

INGREDIENTS

2 ½ ripe bananas
½ cup butter, melted
¾ cup brown sugar
½ cup sugar
2 eggs
2 teaspoons baking soda
1 teaspoon baking powder
2 teaspoons vanilla extract
½ cup plain Greek yogurt
2 cups flour
2 Tablespoons dried lavender

CREATION

a. Preheat oven to 350*F
b. In large mixing bowl, whisk together eggs and sugar until creamy.
c. Add in melted butter, Greek yogurt; whisk together until creamy.
d. Add in baking soda, baking powder, vanilla, add lavender, mix.
e. Add in the mashed banana, mix well.
f. Add in flour until mixed.
g. In baking pan, cupcake pan or bread loaf pan, grease lightly with butter.
h. Add batter to pan, bake for 25-30 minutes until golden and toothpick comes out clean.
i. Let rest until cool, can eat warm, can reheat, tastes delicious with butter on top.

Lavender Banana Bread

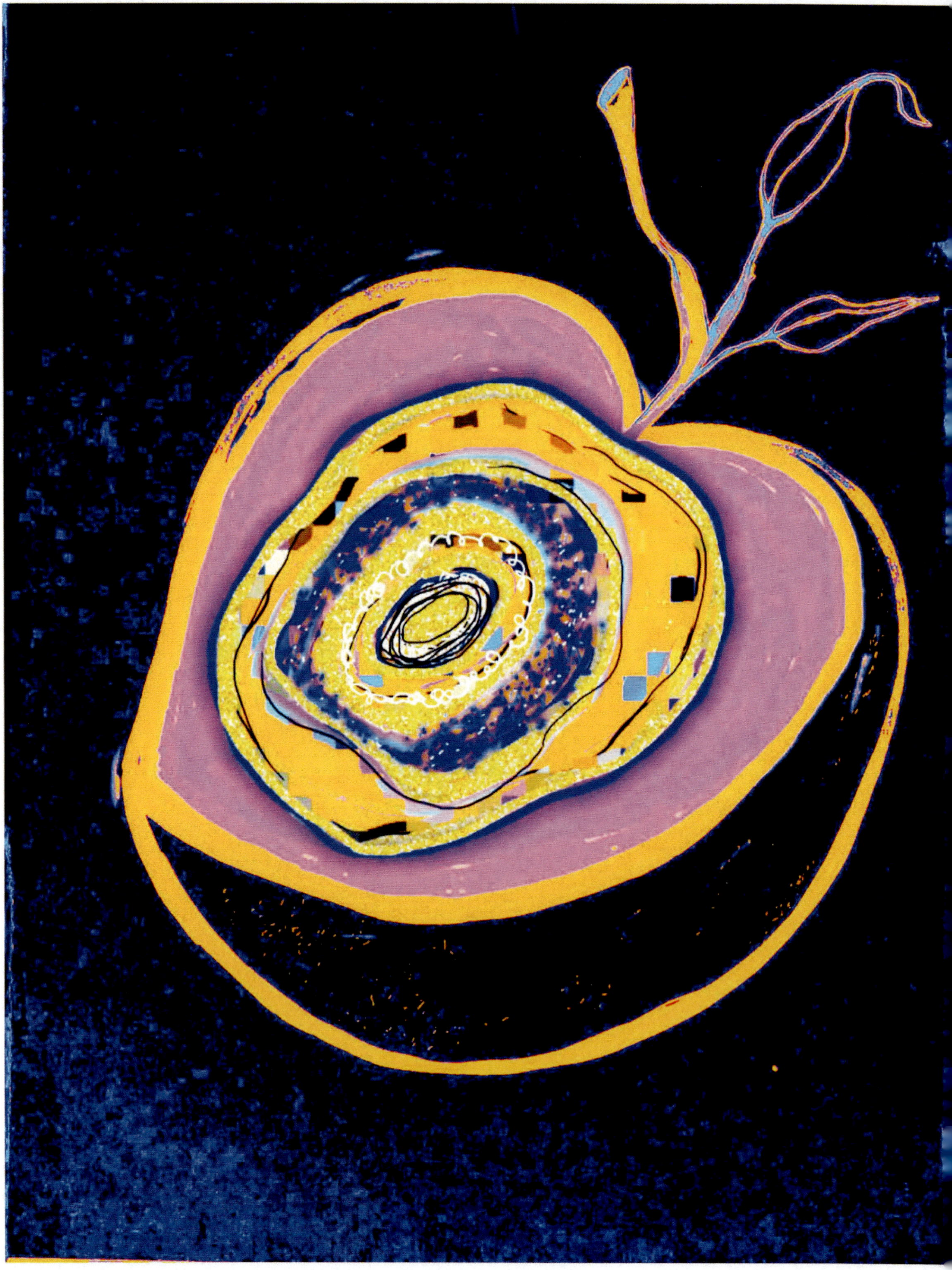

Deo Rocks

PREP TIME: 45 minutes // COOK TIME: 15-20 minutes // YIELD: 8 servings

INGREDIENTS

2 ½ cups flour
2 teaspoons baking powder
¾ teaspoon salt
½ teaspoon baking soda
¾ cup buttermilk
2-3 tablespoons unsalted butter
1 tablespoon onion, diced
1-2 diced apricots, strain liquid

Onion & Apricot Biscuits

CREATION

a. Preheat oven to 425*F

b. In large mixing bowl, mix together, flour, salt, baking soda and baking powder. Add in cold butte, using pastry cutter, cut butter into flour mixture.

c. Add onion and apricot.

d. Remove dough from bowl, knead on top of lightly floured surface, a few times. Do not over knead. Leave dough slightly chunky with butter and a little floured and messy.

e. Roll dough out so it is 2 inches in thickness.

f. Using a round cookie cutter, cut and place on parchment lined baking sheet.

g. Brush buttermilk over surface of biscuit.

h. Bake for 15-18 minutes or until surface becomes lightly golden in color.

Sweet & Spicy Pigments

INGREDIENTS FOR SPICY SALSA

- 1 serrano pepper
- 2 teaspoon salt
- 1 teaspoon pepper
- 1 cup black beans, diced
- 1 habanero
- 1 teaspoon ground red pepper
- 1 teaspoon red chili flakes
- 1 teaspoon black pepper

INGREDIENTS

- 2 habaneros
- cilantro & ripe peaches, peeled and diced
- 1 teaspoon black pepper

For spicy salsa:
b. Quickly sauté peppers and onions, about 2-3 minutes.
- For spicy salsa, add diced tomatoes, mix.
c. Add diced tomatoes over medium heat, just till hot.

Remove from heat.

CREATION

1. Preheat oven to 350°F
2. Prepare streusel topping.
   - skin from peaches and dice, add to mixing bowl
   c. Add salt and pepper, mix well
   d. Refrigerate before serving

Creation for PEACH Picant-so
a. Dice onion, dice cilantro, place in medium/large mixing bowl.
b. Wash, peel

- ½ cup sugar
- 1 teaspoon baking soda
- 1 cup (2 sticks) unsalted butter, room temp 4 eggs
- ½ cup sour cream
- 1 tablespoon vanilla extract

2. Add tomatoes, onion and peppers to bowl, mix in all other ingredients.
Mix well.
Can be stored in airtight jar in refrigerator for up to 1 week.

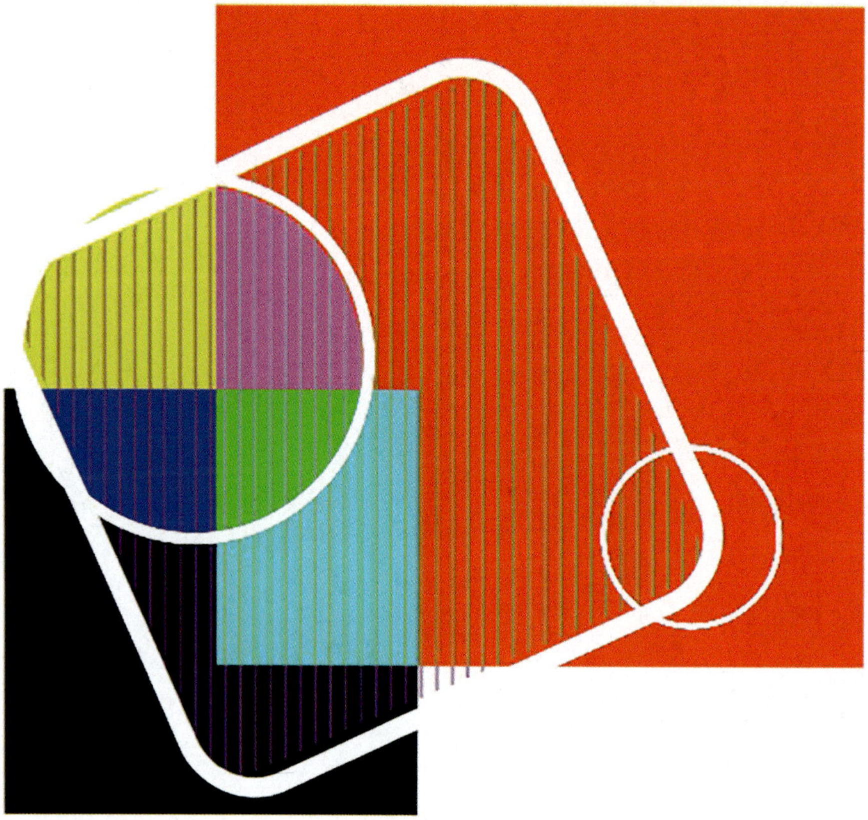

Glued Crackle

PREP TIME: 10 minutes // COOK TIME: 20 minutes // YIELD: 12 servings

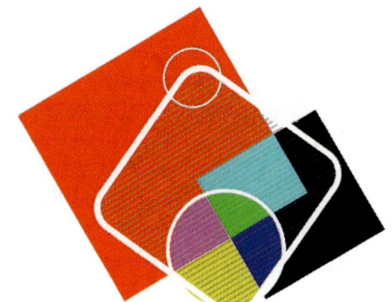

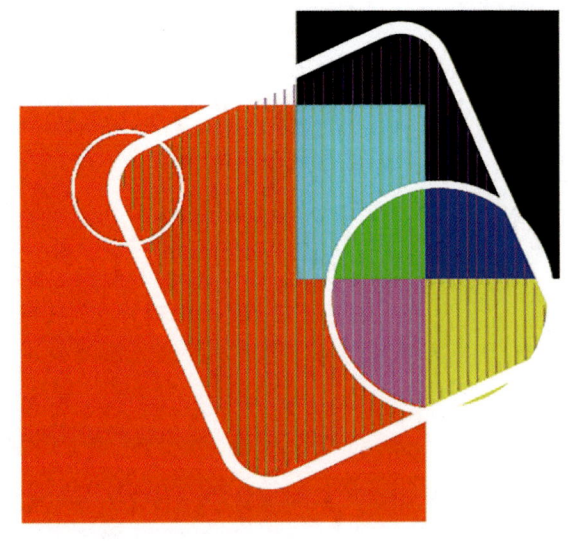

Rosemary & Vanilla Rice Crispy Treats

INGREDIENTS

1 ½ sticks of butter
1 recipe of Fluff Bricks
1 teaspoon vanilla
1 tablespoon fresh rosemary, minced
Pinch salt
8 ½ cups of Rice Krispy Cereal

CREATION

1. Prepare one recipe of fluff bricks, make ahead of time

a. Line baking pan with parchment paper. Lightly grease parchment with coconut oil.
b. Melt butter in medium saucepan, over medium heat.
c. When butter is melted, add fluff bricks to melted butter, stir until fluff bricks and butter are melted together, completely.
d. Remove from heat, add vanilla, rosemary and salt.
e. Add in cereal and mix until all cereal is coated with marshmallow mixture.
f. Transfer it into baking pan and press into pan.
e. Allow treats to sit for a minimum of 1-2 hours before cutting and serving.

Painted Curves

PREP TIME: 15 minutes // COOK TIME: 25 minutes // YIELD: 6-8 servings

INGREDIENTS

1 cup sugar

Peel of 2 oranges

10-15 whole cloves

2 cinnamon sticks

5 whole star anise

3 teaspoons vanilla or two vanilla beans

8 bosc pears (peel the skin off pears leaving stem in place and pears whole

5 cups port wine

INGREDIENTS FOR DRIZZLE

4 baking white chocolate bars, large

2 Vanilla beans

1 teaspoon ground anise

Port & Spice Poached Pears

CREATION

1. **Prepare poaching liquid:**

a. In large saucepan, place all ingredients except pears. Make sure pan is big enough to fit all pears upright in liquid. Make sure that liquid completely covers pears.

b. Bring mixture to a light steam, hot but not quite boiling.

c. Add pears and bring to boil. Allow to boil with pears upright in pan for about 3-4 minutes

d. Turn oven off but leave on burner and leave pears in it. Allow mixture to cool completely.

e. Put mixture in fridge for a few hours, until chilled. If you prefer to eat pears warm. You may eat warm.

2. **Prepare drizzle:**

a. Melt white chocolate

b. Add vanilla and anise. Mix well.

c. Drizzle over top of chilled pears.

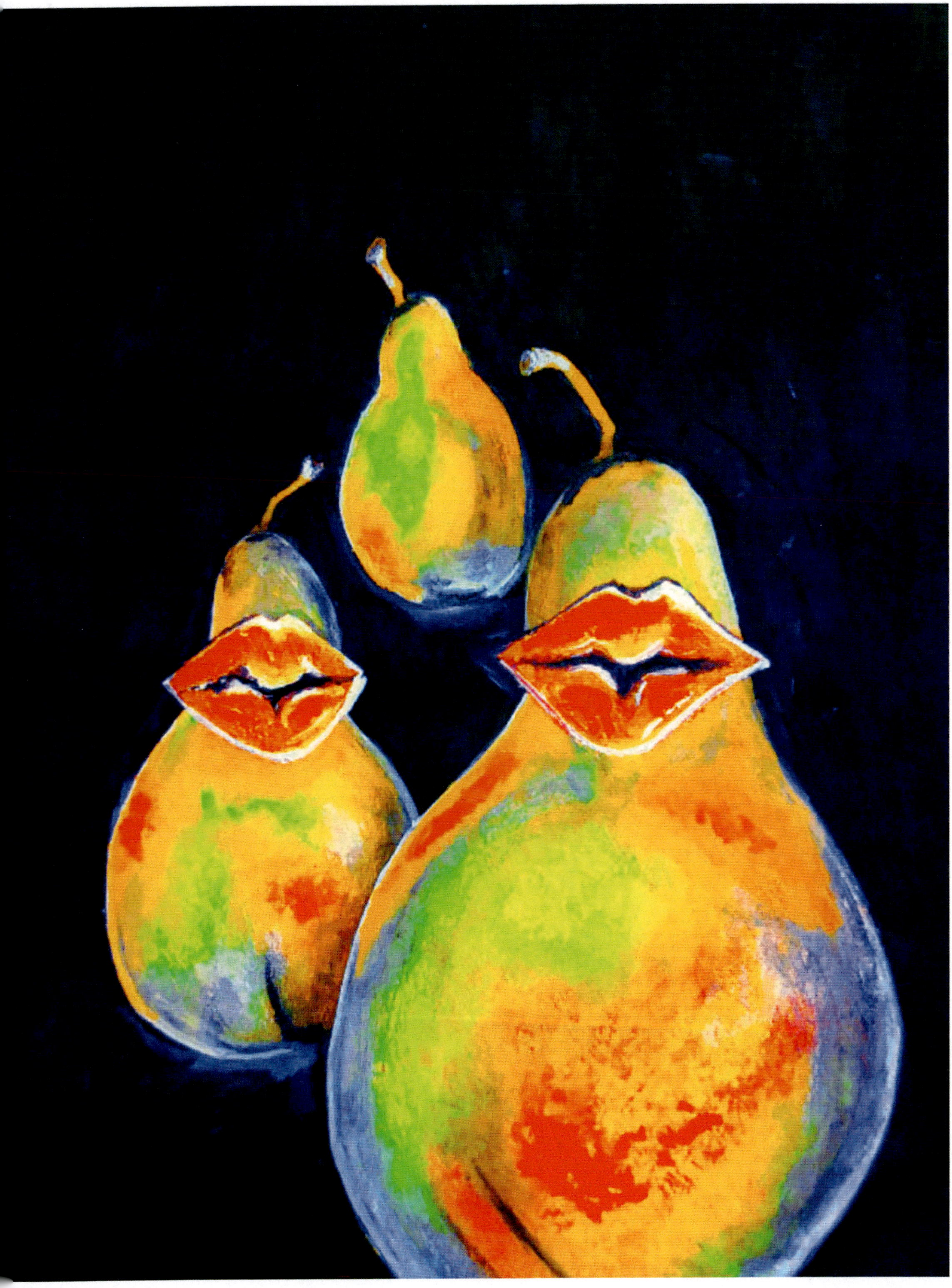

Clayum

PREP TIME: 10 minutes // COOK TIME: 20 minutes // YIELD: 12-24 servings

Lavender Vanilla & Salt Licorice Fudge

INGREDIENTS

3 cups white chocolate chips

14 ounces sweetened condensed milk

2 tablespoon butter

2 vanilla beans

3 tablespoons dried lavender

INGREDIENTS FOR SALT LICORICE

Omit the lavender

Add 2 teaspoons ground star anise

Sprinkle coarse salt on top of fudge

CREATION

a. Line baking pan with parchment paper, even the sides.

b. Add baking chips, condensed milk and butter in medium saucepan over low-medium heat, stirring constantly, until melted.

c. Remove from heat, add vanilla bean and lavender (or if making salt licorice fudge, omit lavender and add star anise).

d. Scoop mixture into baking pan, spread evenly. If its salt licorice fudge, sprinkle coarse salt over entire top.

e. Cool in refrigerator for 3 hours or more, before cutting and serving. Fudge should be firm.

Butter Buttons

PREP TIME: 10-15 minutes // COOK TIME: 10 minutes // YIELD: 12-24 servings

INGREDIENTS

10 tablespoons salted stick butter

½ cup sugar

½ cup powdered sugar

½ cups flour

vanilla bean or 2 teaspoons vanilla

teaspoon butter extract

Vanilla Shortbread Cookies

CREATION

a. In large bowl, cream together the butter and sugar.

b. Add in flour a little at a time, mixing well between.

c. Add vanilla and butter extract.

d. Cover and place in fridge to chill for minimum one hour, until firm.

e. Remove cookie dough from fridge and roll out and shape into desired shape.

f. Place on parchment lined baking sheet.

g. Preheat oven to 350*F

h. While oven is preheating, place cookies in fridge for 10-15 minutes before placing cookies in oven to bake. Cookie dough needs to be cold before baking.

i. Bake about 10 minutes.

j. Remove from oven, remove from cookie sheet and allow cookies to cool on rack.

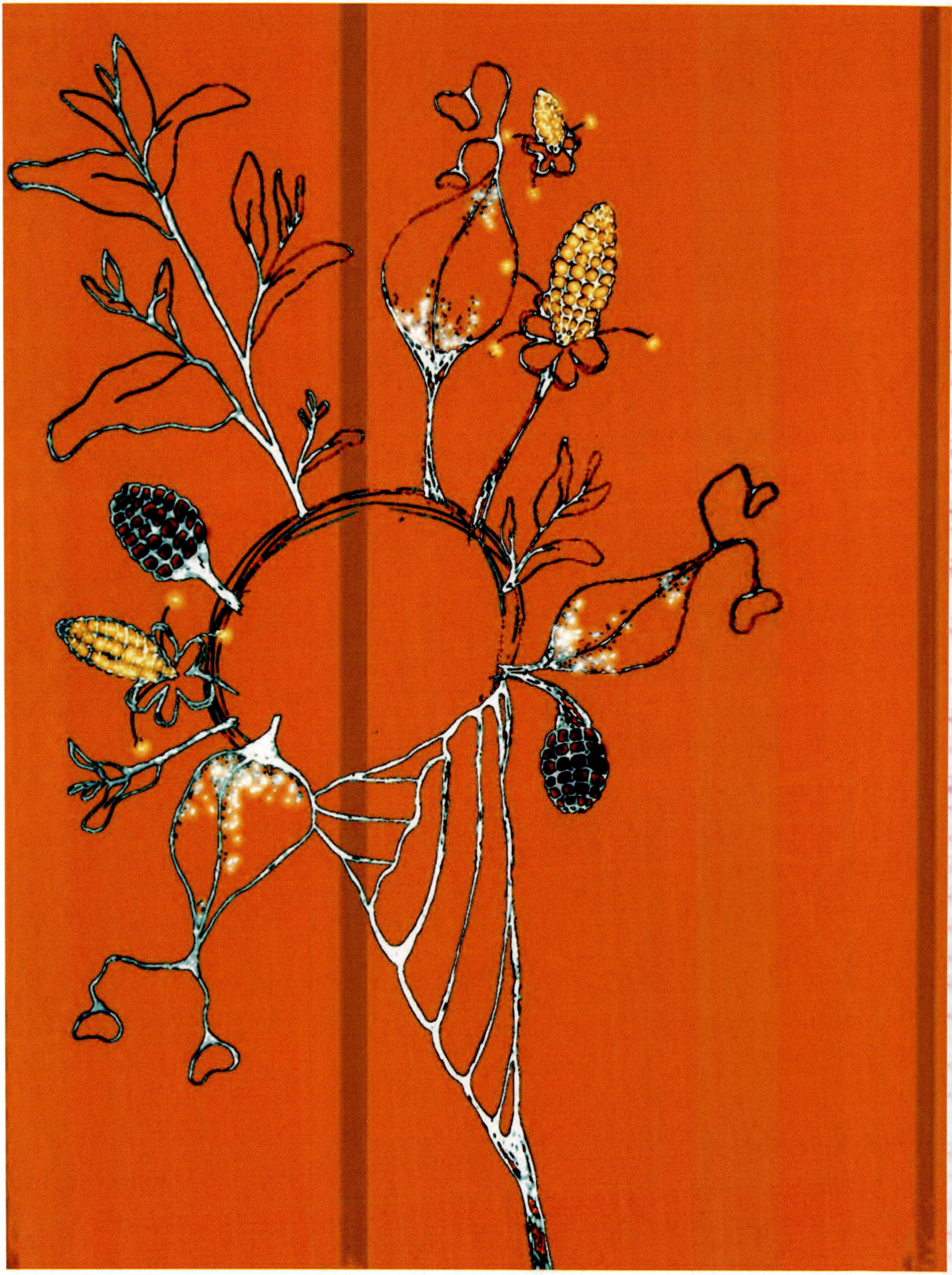

Siberian Blooms

PREP TIME: 15 minutes // COOK TIME: 20-30 minutes // YIELD: 12 Servings

INGREDIENTS

½ cup whole milk
1/2 cups sugar
2 1/2 cups heavy cream
½ teaspoon salt
3 vanilla beans
6 egg yolks

IF making any other flavor except vanilla. See below for added ingredients to create each flavor.

IF making Vanilla Thyme:
a. Prepare as said in creation
b. Add fresh thyme to mixture when hot, removing stems. Mix well.

IF making blackberry sage:
a. Prepare as said in creation
b. Add 1 bunch fresh sage, minced, to mixture when hot.
c. Add 1 cup fresh blackberries, mashed, lightly to mixture prior to freezing

IF making Sweet corn:
a. Prepare as said in creation
b. Add 2 cups sweet cream corn to mixture prior to freezing, mix well
c. Drizzle sweetened condensed milk to top of this ice cream

CREATION

a. In medium saucepan, over medium heat, combine milk, sugar and heavy cream.
b. Cut and scrape vanilla bean. Set aside.
c. Cook until the mixture is hot, thoroughly, not boiling. Stirring often to prevent from burning milk.
d. Add vanilla bean to mixture, turn heat off. Let mixture steep for at least 20-30 minutes.
e. Pour in heavy cream to mixture.
f. In a separate bowl, whisk the egg yolks. While whisking, pour the vanilla bean mixture slowly into the eggs, whisky constantly. Until all mixture has been whisked in. Do NOT do this process too fast, as you don't want the egg yolk cooked.
g. Place the saucepan back on the heat, medium heat. Whisking constantly making sure to scrape the bottom as you stir, to keep from burning. Cook until the mixture thickens. It should be able to coat the back of a spoon without dripping off.
h. Pour the mixture through a strainer into glass bowl or jar, once all mixture has been strained, cover, sealing mixture completely. Place in freezer until firm. Usually overnight.

Vanilla Thyme
Blackberry Sage
Sweet Corn
Ice Cream

Mi Craft Blocks

PREP TIME: 10 minutes // COOK TIME: 30 minutes // YIELD: 12 servings

Brownies Avocado Frosting

INGREDIENTS

1 1/4 cup butter, melted
½ cup unsweetened cocoa powder
2 cups flour
1 ¾ cup sugar
4 eggs
1 tablespoon vanilla

INGREDIENTS FOR AVOCADO FROSTING

1/4 cup milk
¼ cup unsweetened cocoa powder
3 cups powdered sugar
1 avocado, mashed

CREATION

a. Preheat oven to 350* F.
b. Line a 9x13 baking pan with coconut oil, set aside.
c. In large bowl, add egg and sugar, cream together.
d. Add melted butter and vanilla, mix well.
e. Add flour and mix until smooth.
f. Add mixture to baking pan. Spread evenly.
g. Bake for 20-25 minutes or until toothpick inserted, comes out clean.

While brownies are baking:

a. Remove skin and seed from avocado, mash.
b. Add cocoa powder, powdered sugar and milk to bowl, mix well.
c. Add to brownies 10 minutes after brownies are removed from oven, but while they are still warm.

Fluff Bricks

PREP TIME: 20 minutes // COOK TIME: 20 minutes // YIELD: 12-24 servings

Rosemary & Vanilla Marshmallows

INGREDIENTS

3 Envelopes of gelatin, non-flavored
½ cup water, cold
1 ¾ cup sugar
2/3 cup light corn syrup
¼ cup water
Pinch of salt
Confectioners' sugar
2 tablespoons vanilla extract or paste from 2 vanilla beans

CREATION

a. Line a cake pan with plastic wrap and lightly oil surface, I use coconut oil, it tastes better.
b. Mix gelatin and cold water in bowl and let sit for about 10 minutes.
c. In medium saucepan, combine sugar, corn syrup and ¼ cup water, whisk until sugar is dissolved. Bring to a boil.
d. Allow it to boil for 1 minute, then remove from heat and slowly and carefully pour the boiling mixture over gelatin mixture, whisking continuously.
e. Add salt, continue whisking until mixture is light and fluffy in consistency.
f. Add vanilla extract or vanilla bean paste.
g. Oil hands with coconut oil and rubber scrapper or spatula. Press into pan so mixture is even.
h. Take a sheet of plastic wrap and lightly oil one side and press that side face down on top of marshmallows. This creates a seal.
i. Let marshmallows sit for a few hours, until completely cooled and set, firmly.
j. Sprinkle a surface with confectioners' sugar and flip marshmallows onto that surface. Completely cover remaining surfaces of marshmallows with confectioners' sugar.
k. Cut marshmallows to desired size, 1x1 inch are a really good size. Toss each marshmallow in confectioners' sugar, coating each side with the sugar.
l. Store in sealed bag or airtight container.

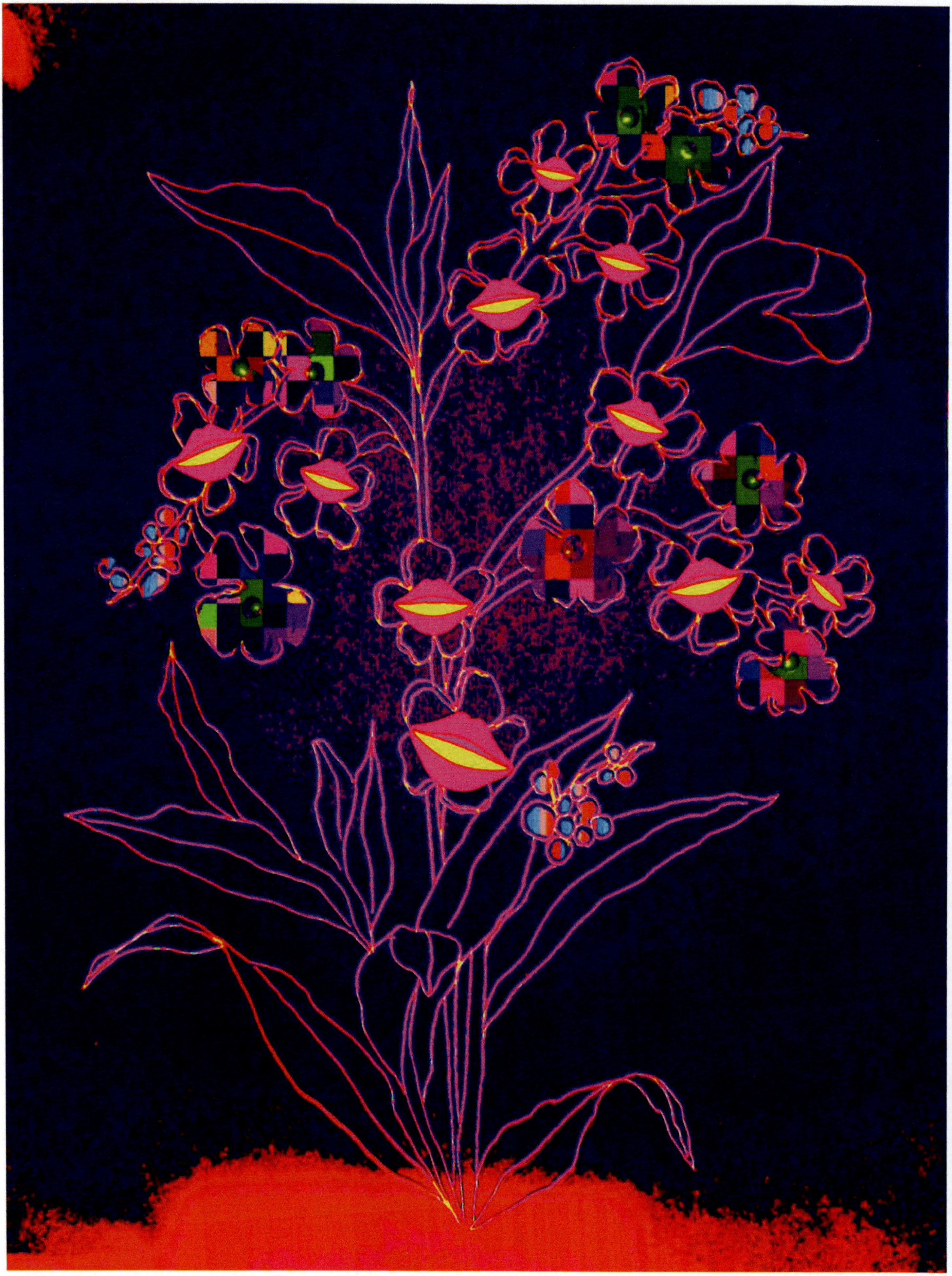

Floral Bites

PREP TIME: 15 minutes // COOK TIME: 8-12 minutes // YIELD: 6-8 servings

Lavender Chocolate Chip Cookies

INGREDIENTS

2 1/4 cups flour
¾ teaspoon baking soda
1 cup salted butter
1 cup packed light brown sugar
½ cup sugar
1 tablespoon vanilla or 2 vanilla beans
1 egg
1 egg yolk
1 ½ cups chocolate chips
3-4 tablespoons dried lavender

CREATION

a. In large bowl, cream together eggs and sugars.
b. Add melted butter.
c. Add baking soda and vanilla and mix well.
d. Add lavender and chocolate chips.
e. Adding flour a little at a time until well mixed.
f. Line cookie sheet with parchment paper.
g. Scoop 2x2in sized cookie dough balls and place 2in apart from one another, evenly on the pan.
h. Place sheet with dough in fridge to cool for 20 minutes.
i. Preheat oven to 325*F.
j. Bake cookies 8-12 minutes, until edges of cookies are golden.
k. Remove from oven, leave on cookie sheet for minute or two, then move cookies to cool on wire rack.

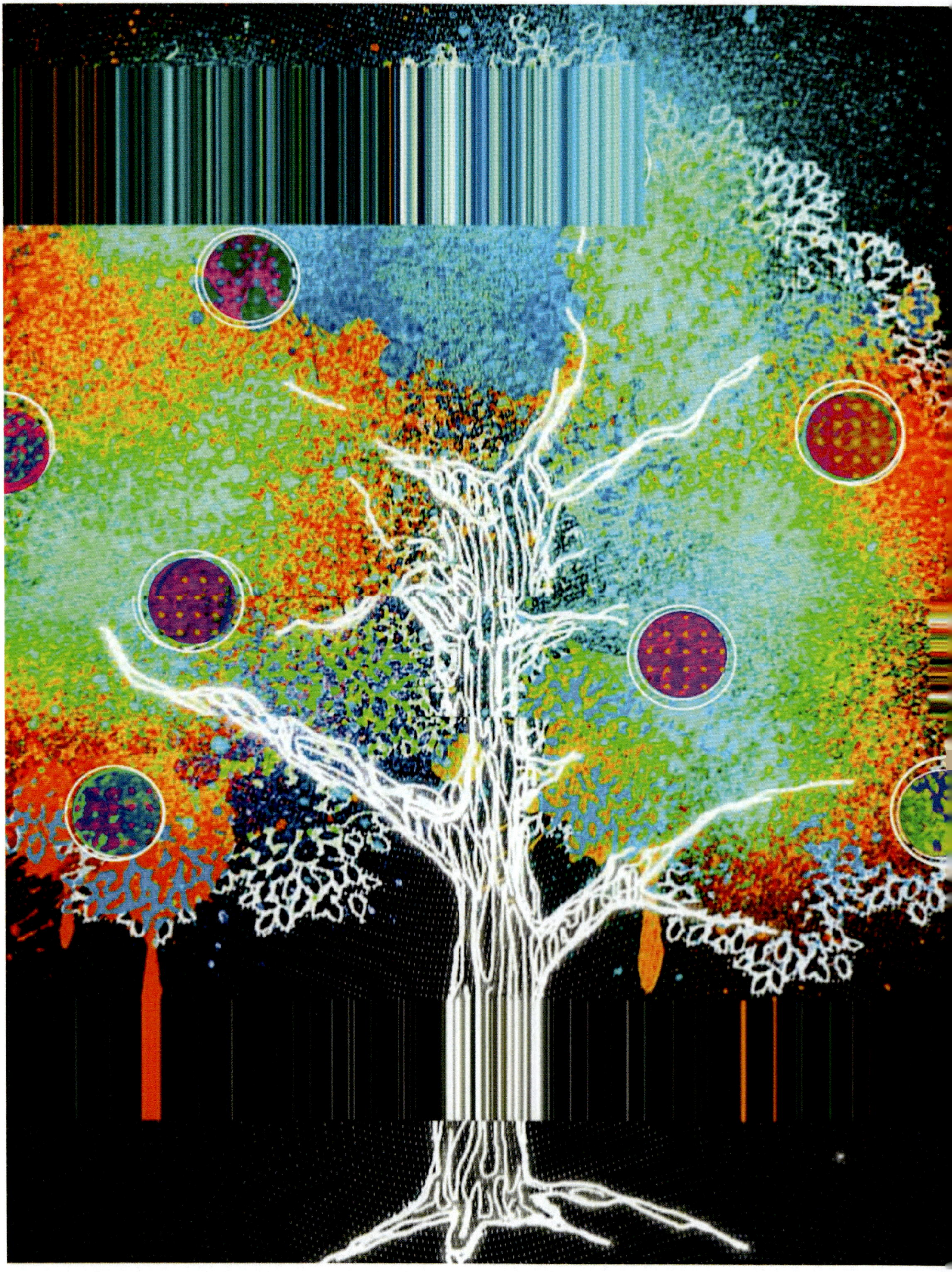

Spiked Tree

Sage & Apple Tart

PREP TIME: 15 minutes // COOK TIME: 35-45 minutes // YIELD: 6-8 Servings

INGREDIENTS

1 ½ stick butter (salted)
¾ cup coconut flour
¾ cup flour
½ cup sugar
1 vanilla bean
½ teaspoon clove
1 ½ teaspoons cardamom
4-5 honey crisp apples, thinly sliced
Zest of 1 lemon
1 teaspoon rum extract
½ teaspoon ginger
3 teaspoons ground sage
1 Empty stage
Recipe on page

CREATION

1. Prepare empty stage recipe (pie dough) ahead of time. Set aside.

2. Prepare tart filling:

a. Mix together: all ingredients in large bowl, except apples.

b. Slice apples, thin. Leaving skin on apples

c. Line pie pan with empty stage dough, then stack upright overlapping each apple to another. Until entire pan is filled with apples.

d. Preheat oven to 400*F.

e. Bake in oven for 30-40 minutes, do not over bake. Remove when apples are tender, and dough is GBD (golden brown delicious).

f. Serve warm or serve with Siberian bloom recipes: Vanilla thyme or blackberry Sage.

CREATION

1. Prepare Deo Rock recipe
   Make apricot and onion deo rock recipe, but do not bake. Add the biscuit dough to soup later on while...

2. Prepare soup
   a. In large pot, add large diced chicken and butter, cook until chicken is nearly cooked thoroughly.
   b. Add celery, shallot and carrots and cook over medium heat for 5 minutes.
   c. Add stock. If you need more liquid, you may add more stock or water. Add bay leaves.
   d. Bring to a boil, then reduce heat to medium low.
   e. Add drops of deo rocks (apricot and onion biscuit dough) to hot soup, roughly ½ inch by ½ inch sized pieces. Cook until biscuit dough is fully cooked. f. Remove bay leaves. Add salt, pepper and paprika; serve hot.

Brined Harvest

PREP TIME: 10 minutes // COOK TIME: 45 minutes // YIELD: 6-8 servings

INGREDIENTS

- 2 fresh whole jalapeños
- 1 fresh habanero
- 2 cups sugar
- 3 fresh pickling cucumbers
- 2 cups water
- 3 cups red Lentils
- 6 medjool dates, whole, pitted
- 3 tablespoons pickling spice

INGREDIENTS FOR PICKLING LIQUID

- 2 cups distilled white vinegar

ARTISTIC FLOW

Lentils & Dates CREATION

1. Prepare pickled brine
   a. In large saucepan, add sugar, water and vinegar, bring to a boil.
   b. while pickling liquid comes to a boil. In a large jar(s), add pickling spices. If using more than one jar, use the same amount of pickling spices per jar. c. Add whole jalapenos, cucumber and habanero to jars.
   d. When pickling liquid comes to boil, remove from heat, pour over vegetables in jars until completely emerged in liquid. Put lid on jar and refrigerate until cool.

2. Prepare lentils
   a. Rinse lentils well.
   b. In large saucepan, fill halfway, ¾ full of water, bring to a boil.

Melted Bricks

PREP TIME: 10 minutes // COOK TIME: 25 minutes // YIELD: 6-8 servings

INGREDIENTS

½ cup dry white wine

½ cup white wine vinegar

2/3 cup heavy cream

3 tablespoons shallot, diced

½ teaspoon salt

½ teaspoon white pepper

3 ½ sticks butter, small cubes

1 ½ tablespoon matcha powder

CREATION

a. In medium saucepan, sauté shallots for 2 minutes, add wine and wine vinegar, boil over medium heat. Reducing liquid for about 5-7 minutes.

b. Add in heavy cream, stir. Reduce heat.

c. Add cubes of butter, a couple at a time, until all butter has been added. Butter should be melted completely.

d. Add matcha powder, cook on low for a couple minutes.

e. Remove from heat, add salt and pepper.

Matcha Buerre Blanc

Spiked Paint

PREP TIME: 15 minutes // COOK TIME: 0 minutes // YIELD: 6-8 servings

Anise & Thyme Beer Batter

INGREDIENTS

1 cup flour
1 teaspoon paprika
2 teaspoons salt
1 teaspoon white pepper
1 ½ cups Ale beer
2 large, sweet Vidalia onions
2 large egg whites
Oil for frying
2 teaspoons fresh thyme
1 teaspoon ground anise

CREATION

a. In large bowl, mix dry ingredients, flour, salt, pepper and paprika, ground anise and finely chopped thyme.

b. Whisk ale beer into mixture until smooth, if mixture seems too thick, add a little more beer.

c. In separate bowl, whisk egg whites until stiff peaks form. d. Fold egg whites into beer batter until mixed but, do not over mix.

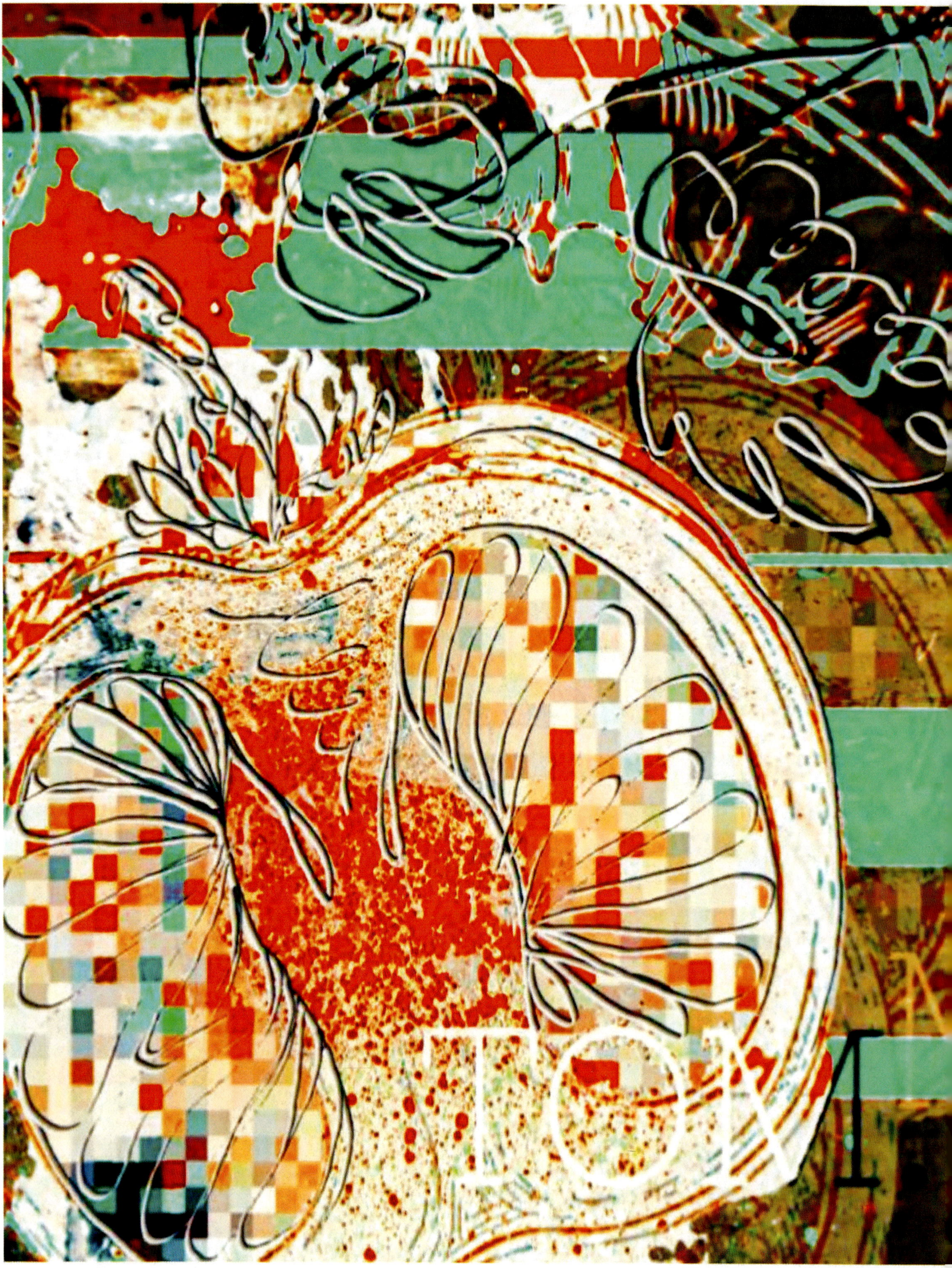

Pigment

PREP TIME: 10 minutes // COOK TIME: 20 minutes // YIELD: 6-8 servings

INGREDIENTS

6 large whole tomatoes, diced
1 medium onion, diced
2 cups fresh pancetta, diced
2 cups fresh basil, whole leaves
1 ½ teaspoons crushed red pepper
1 ½ teaspoons salt

Basil & Pancetta Tomato Sauce

CREATION

a. In medium saucepan, add diced pancetta. Cook until slightly crispy.

b. Add diced onion, sauté until onions are soft.

c. Add diced tomatoes, bring to a boil, then reduce heat to low and simmer sauce until tomatoes break down and become more sauce-like.

d. Add crushed pepper, salt and fresh basil, cook until basil wilts.

e. Remove from heat.

TopCoat *Simple Syrup*

PREP TIME: 5 minutes // COOK TIME: 15 minutes // YIELD: 6 Servings

INGREDIENTS

3 cups white sugar
2 cups water

Vanilla syrup:
Add 2 pastes of vanilla bean

Anise syrup:
Add 1 teaspoon ground anise
or 1 teaspoon anise extract

CREATION

a. In medium saucepan, whisk water and sugar until sugar dissolves.

b. Cook over medium heat, whisking often, until mixture comes to a boil.

c. Boil mixture for 7-10 minutes. Remove from heat, allowing syrup to cool slightly and thicken, add vanilla or anise to mixture and mix well.

ModdguePodge

PREP TIME: 10 minutes // COOK TIME: 25 minutes // YIELD: 6 Servings

INGREDIENTS

½ cup butter
½ cup flour
2 ½ cups half and half
1 teaspoon salt
1 teaspoon white pepper
4 tablespoons fresh or ground sage

White Sage Gravy

CREATION

a. In medium saucepan, combine butter and flour, whisking continuously to make a roux. Cook until mixture does not stick to sides of pan.

b. Adding in a little at a time, whisking constantly, add in half and half, until all half and half has eventually been added. Cook until mixture is thick like gravy and smooth in texture.

c. If it is too thick, add a little more half and half.

d. Remove from heat, add salt, pepper and sage.

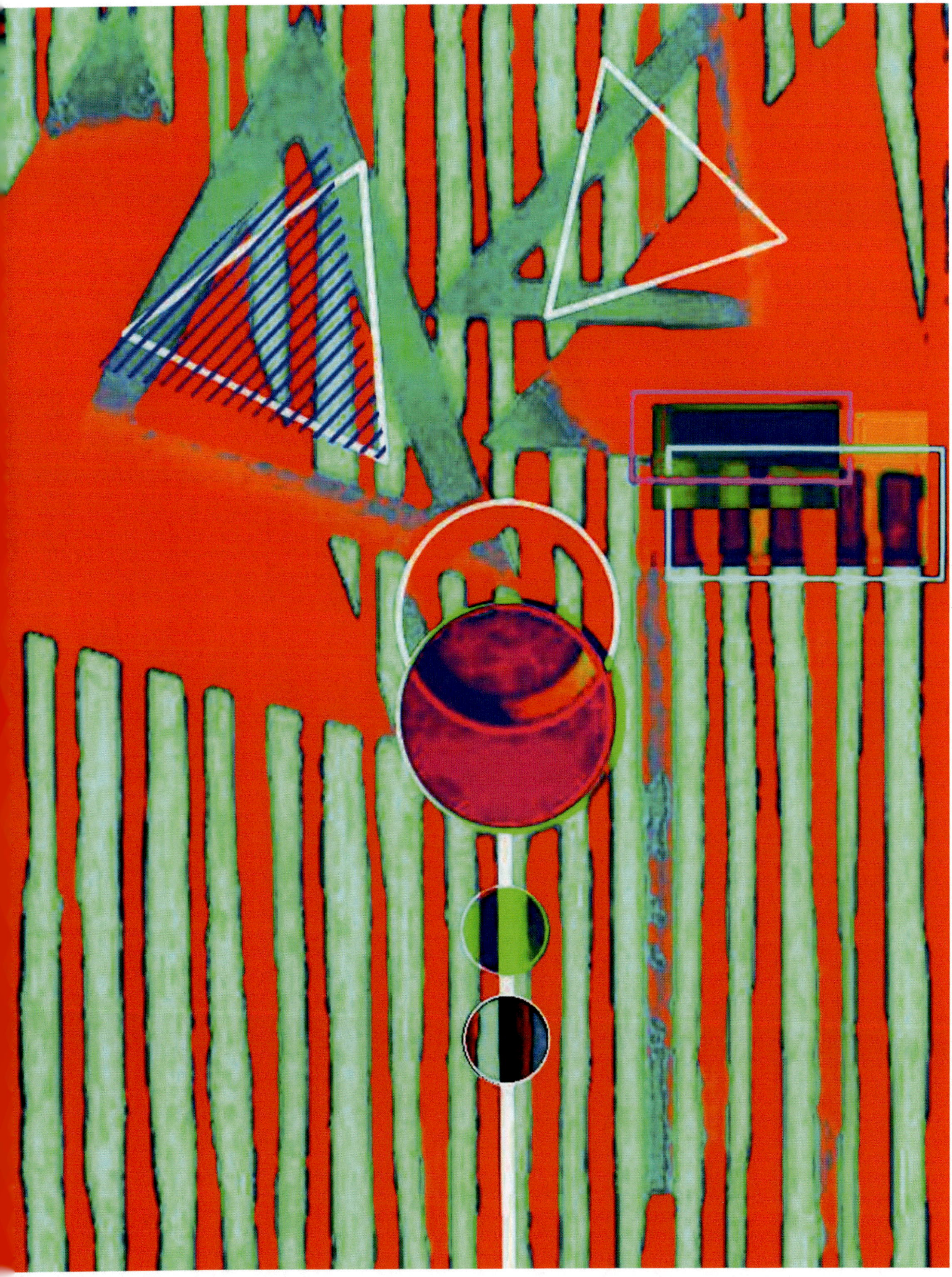

White out

PREP TIME: 10 minutes // COOK TIME: 20 minutes // YIELD: 6-8 servings

White Wine Bechamel Fennel & Shallot

INGREDIENTS

6 tablespoon butter
¼ cup flour
3 ½ cups half & half
1 ½ teaspoons salt
1 teaspoon white pepper
½ teaspoon ground nutmeg
½ cup shallot, diced
½ cup finely sliced fennel

CREATION

a. Dice shallot and fennel, place in saucepan with white wine and sauté until onions are soft and white wine cooks down a bit.
b. Add butter and flour to make roux.
c. Cook butter and flour mixture, stirring constantly until flour has cooked and butter and flour mixture makes a ball that does not stick to the pan.
d. Whisking continuously, adding a small amount at a time, add half and half, until all half and half has been added.
e. Continue to cook until mixture is creamy and thick in texture.
f. Remove from heat, add salt, pepper and nutmeg, mix. Keep bechamel warm for serving.

Butter Glue

PREP TIME: 25 minutes // COOK TIME: 20 minutes // YIELD: 6-8 servings

Ginger & Vanilla Flour Frosting

INGREDIENTS

¾ cup flour

2 tablespoons cornstarch

Pinch of salt

2 cups sugar

2 cups whole milk

2 cups butter, cubed

2 tsp vanilla

½ teaspoon ground ginger

CREATION

a. In medium saucepan, add sugar, cornstarch, flour and milk to saucepan. Heat and stir constantly on medium heat.
b. Cook until mixture become thick, like gravy.
c. Remove from heat, add vanilla and place in large mixing bowl. Cover with plastic wrap, directly on the mixture, to prevent film from forming cool to room temperature.
d. Once mixture has been cooled to room temperature, using hand mixer or electric mixer, whisk mixture until it becomes fluffy in texture.
e. While mixing consistently, slowly add a few cubes of butter to mixture, until fluffy. Continue adding a few cubes at a time and whisking until fluffy before adding new cubes in.
f. Once all cubes of butter are added, whisk more to ensure that frosting is fluffy and thicker.
g. Mix in ground ginger and whisk until well mixed.

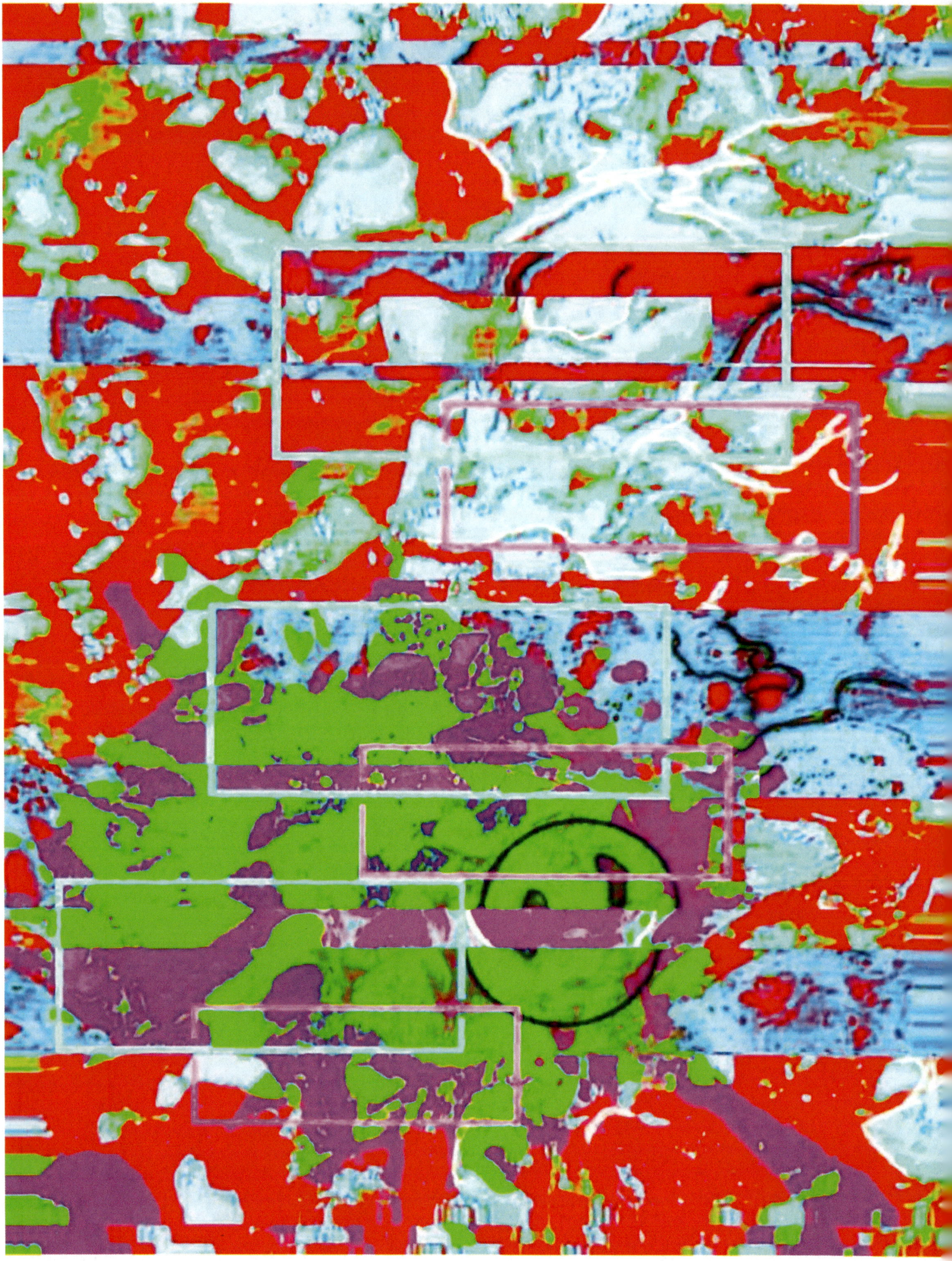

Picant-So

PREP TIME: 15 minutes // COOK TIME: 15 minutes // YIELD: 6-8 Servings

INGREDIENTS

8-10 Ripe tomatoes
1 yellow onion
2 jalapenos
1 bunch fresh cilantro
1 garlic clove
Zest of 2 limes
Juice from 1 lime
1 Anaheim/poblano pepper
1 teaspoon ground cumin
2 bell peppers (any color)
2 serrano peppers
2 teaspoons salt
1 teaspoon pepper
1 cup black beans

INGREDIENTS FOR SPICY SALSA

2 habaneros
1 teaspoon ground red pepper
1 teaspoon red chili flakes

INGREDIENTS FOR PEACH SALSA

1 yellow onion,
1 bunch of cilantro
6 ripe peaches, peeled and diced
1 teaspoon black pepper
½ teaspoon salt

CREATION

1. Preparing for REGULAR/SPICY Picant-so

a. Remove all stems and seeds from peppers. Dice onion, tomatoes.

b. Quickly sauté peppers and onions, about 2-3 minutes.

• For spicy salsa, add the habaneros to mix.

c. Add diced tomatoes over medium heat, just till hot. Remove from heat.

d. Add tomatoes, onion and peppers to bowl, mix in all other ingredients. Mix well.

e. Cool until ready to eat. Can be stored in airtight jar in refrigerator for up to 1 week.

2. Creation for PEACH Picant-so:

a. Dice onion, dice cilantro, place in medium/large mixing bowl.

b. Wash, peel skin from peaches and dice, add to mixing bowl.

c. Add salt and pepper, mix well.

d. Refrigerate before serving.

Salsa

Sunkiss

PREP TIME: 5 minutes // COOK TIME: 0 minutes // YIELD: 6 Servings

INGREDIENTS

3 tablespoons white wine vinegar

½ cup blood orange juice

2/3 cup olive oil

1 tablespoon diced shallots

1 tablespoon diced chives

Zest of one ,blood orange

1 tablespoon honey

CREATION

a. Combine all ingredients, in jar and shake until ingredients have emulsified together.

Blood Orange Vinaigrette

Molten Lava *Chocolate Gravy*

PREP TIME: 10 minutes // COOK TIME: 20 minutes // YIELD: 6 Servings

INGREDIENTS

1/3 cup unsweetened cocoa powder

4 tablespoons flour

¾ cup sugar

¼ cup brown sugar

1 ¾ cup half and half

4 tablespoons butter

2 teaspoons vanilla extract or

1 vanilla bean

Pinch of salt

CREATION

a. Melt half butter in medium saucepan over medium heat.

b. Add cocoa powder, flour and sugars and pinch of salt into medium saucepan, whisk, making a roux. Cook a couple minutes to cook flour down.

c. Slowly add half and half, until all-of the half and half is used and added.

d. Whisking constantly, over medium heat, until sauce thickens.

e. Once sauce is thick, add remaining butter and vanilla. Mix until butter is melted.

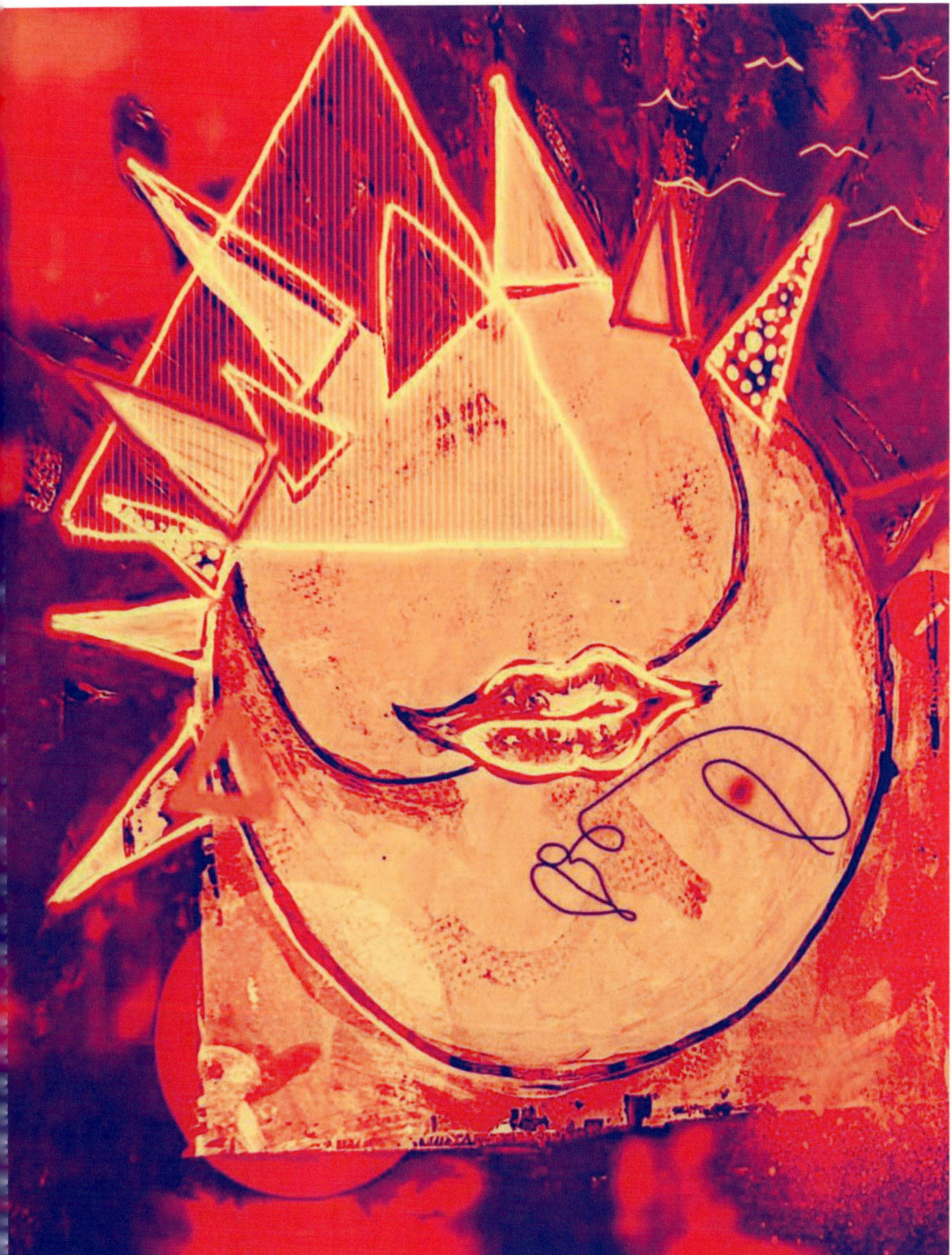

INDEX

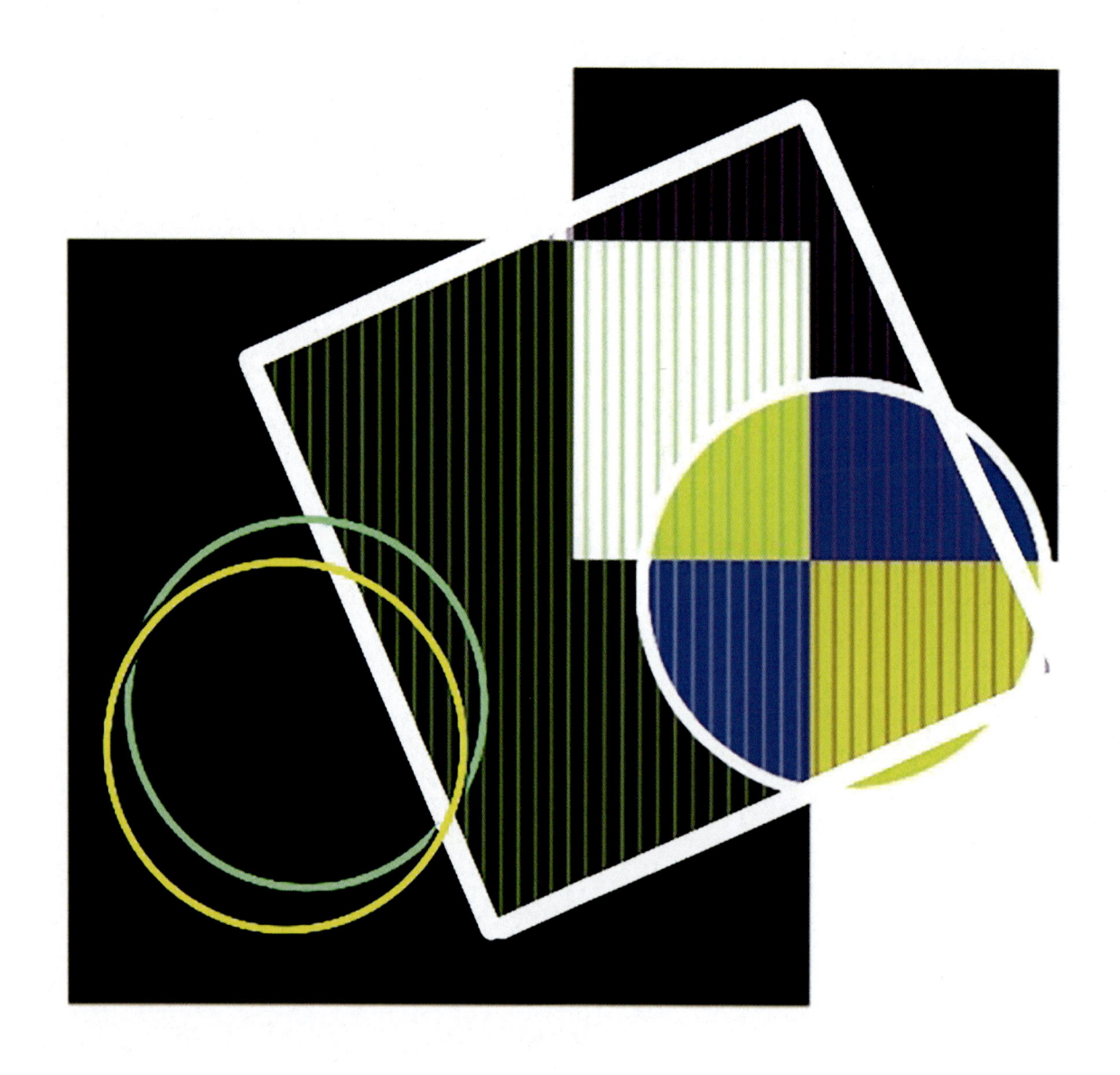

Quick-Find ME!

Artama-zing	27
Artistic Plateau	69
Bak & Clouds	28
Blistered Scrafts	43
Blue Desert	31
Brined Harvest	53
Brown Globes	19
Butter Buttons	104
Butter Glue	122
Calming Banana Board	94
Circular Canvases	90
Citrus Felt	23
Citrus Sponge Branch	84
Clayum	103

Quick Find ME!

Coastal Mounds & Moddguepodge	48
Coastal Twisters	79
Cubed Tart Globe	20
Deo Rocks	96
Dew Platable Nara	68
Dressed Cobs	51
Drunken Sprouts	42
Earth Capsacity	16
Empty Stage	83
European Mud Pies	73
Floral Bites	110
Fluff Bricks	108
Forest & Bulbs	73
Frizzled Greens	50

Quick-Find ME!

Ginger & the Beanstock	36
Glued Crackle	100
Greens & Clay	37
Herbed Layers	47
Kristine's Masterpiece	66
Lotus	33
Marked Canvaloupe & Salty Paper	17
Melted Bricks	115
Mi-Craft Blocks	107
Mini Palettes	14
Moddgue Podge	119
Moddgue Rocks	59
Molten Lava	125
Mossed Ocean & Tart Seeds	71

Quick-Find ME!

Mossy Hearts	23
Mud Pies	60
Painted Curves	101
Painted Sunset	77
Panned Stalks	50
Pansta	67
Picant-so	124
Pigment	118
Plateau	92
Pop-Ert	35
Prism of Colors	31
Pungent Circles	22
Quick Sand	63
Rolled Canvas	62

Quick-Find ME!

Savory Flowers	42
Scarlet River Beads	80
Shells in the Clouds	30
Siberian Blooms	106
Silky Pearls	44
Sir Fermented	76
Skipped Sidewalk Knots	85
Spiked Paint	116
Spiked Tree	112
Sunkiss	125
Sun-Out	57
Sweet & Spicy Grounds	87
Sweet Roots	46
Sweet Vibes	37

Quick-Find ME!

TopCoat	119
Tri-canvases & Picant-so	17
Turkish Brealight	89
White Out	121

More Sketchy Kitchen in creation...